BEST SHORT HIKES

IN WASHINGTON'S

NORTH CASCADES & SAN JUAN ISLANDS

E. M. STERLING

PHOTOS BY BOB & IRA SPRING

THE
MOUNTAINEERS

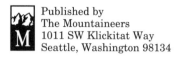 Published by
The Mountaineers
1011 SW Klickitat Way
Seattle, Washington 98134

Published simultaneously in Canada by Douglas & McIntyre, Ltd. 1615
Venables Street, Vancouver, B.C. V5L 2H1

Published simultaneously in Great Britain by Cordee
3a DeMontfort Street, Leicester, England, LE1 7HD

Manufactured in the United States of America

Edited by Dana Fos
Maps by Brian Metz/Green Rhino Graphics
Photographs by Bob and Ira Spring; photos on pages 53, 60, 88, 97, and 103 by
    John Spring
Cover design by Watson Graphics
Book design and typesetting by The Mountaineers Books

Cover photograph: Mount Baker and hiker on Skyline Trail (Photo by Bob and
    Ira Spring)

Library of Congress Cataloging-in-Publication Data
Sterling, E. M.
    Best short hikes in Washington's North Cascades and San Juan Islands
/ by E. M. Sterling ; photos by Bob and Ira Spring.
        p.   cm.
    Includes index.
    ISBN 0-89886-382-1
    1. Hiking--Washington (State)--Guidebooks. 2. Hiking--
Washington (State)--San Juan Islands--Guidebooks. 3. Hiking--
Cascade Range--Guidebooks. 4. Washington (State)--Guidebooks.
6. Cascade Range--Guidebooks.
    I. Title.
GV199.42.W2S74   1993
796.5'1'09797--dc20   93-41781
                                                                    CIP

Contents

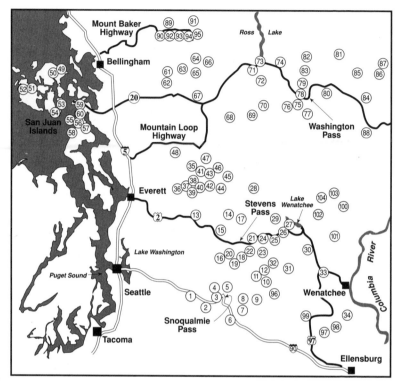

Mountain Loop Highway
(Granite Falls to Darrington)

North Cascades Highway 20
(San Juan Islands to Twisp)

Mount Baker Highway 542
(Glacier to Artist Point)

Highway 97
(Cle Elum to Entiat)

Introduction

This book was put together specifically for all those lovers of the Northwest outdoors who savor the nature and beauty of this area but who, for whatever reason, must limit their time or energy to hours, at the least, or full days, at the most.

Offered here are hikes, with few exceptions, of 2 miles or less—some easy, some difficult—to waterfalls, meadows, ancient forests, lakes, lookouts, rivers, ridges, beaver ponds, and seashores. All of them are found in the parks and forests along major highways and ferry routes from Seattle north through the San Juan Islands to Canada and south to the Columbia River, with each hike offering a prime example, in its own way, of the best the Northwest has to offer, whether just inside the boundaries of a wilderness or park or surrounded on every side by clearcuts.

Some of the hikes, such as those on formal nature trails, require little time or energy. Some even offer wheelchair access. Most of the hikes make moderate demands on the hiker. A number are downright difficult. But all of them are worth whatever effort you put into them, even if you must turn back before you finish.

The hikes were selected with everyone in mind: The permanent residents who must provide outdoor samples of the Northwest to visiting friends and relatives. The temporary residents—students, workers, businesspeople, convention-goers—who seek quick samples of the beauty of the Northwest. The newcomers who cannot wait to explore the outdoor wonders that suddenly surround them. The physically limited, both young and old, who seek short hikes to places they feel only the able have been permitted to enjoy. Those among us who fear mountains, but know that they should not. And those many, many more who already know and love this area but seek one more place to spend a day or afternoon resampling the nature and beauty they've already learned to enjoy.

The format here is simple. The hikes are listed in order along major cross-state highways. Each hike is conveniently described,

Pride Basin from road beyond Sloan Creek Campground (Hike 45)

pictured, and, in most instances, mapped on facing pages. Driving directions are complete for each hike. Larger maps in the Green Trails series are identified. The Appendix lists nearby campgrounds along all of the major highway routes.

Equipment

Equipment needs for all of these hikes are minimal. Although street shoes will suffice on some of the "easy" trails listed here, hiking shoes are recommended for all of them, because all mountain trails can be rough, sometimes muddy, and even slippery.

Every hiker in the mountains, even on the short hikes listed here, should start every hike prepared, in an emergency, to survive for at least the night. Accidents occur in mountains, as in the city, without warning. But in the mountains often no one is nearby to help. There is no 911 to call.

The Mountaineers' list of Ten Essentials should be carried on every hiking trip:

1. Extra clothing
2. Extra food
3. Sunglasses
4. Knife
5. Firestarter
6. First-aid kit
7. Matches in a waterproof container
8. Flashlight
9. Map
10. Compass—and the knowledge to use it

All should fit in a rucksack, certainly. And yes, take your camera and, if you have them, a flower book, a bird book, and pictures of animal tracks. See Reading Suggestions.

Maps

Although Green Trails maps are identified for most trails in this book, maps prepared by each national forest will provide a broader view. Such maps can be purchased at ranger stations or at many outdoor equipment stores. Areas here embrace Mount Baker–Snoqualmie, Okanogan, and Wenatchee national forests and North Cascades National Park.

Water

Take water, too. None of the water in any of the streams crossed on these trails, tragically, should nowadays be considered safe to drink. If you must use water from a stream, it should be brought to a rolling boil for 20 minutes, filtered through any of several approved systems offered by outdoor equipment stores, or treated with iodine as directed on packages offered, again, by established outdoor equipment stores.

Newborn fawn

Fires

On these short hikes campfires are discouraged. Most of the destinations here where campfires might suggest themselves are already overused and, for firewood, overcut. If you want hot soup or coffee for lunch, carry a small mountain stove, not only to warm your meal but also to save your destination from further destruction.

Trash and Waste

By all means carry out whatever trash you carry in, such as paper, bottles, and cans. And if you truly want to help, carry out what others may have left.

Use trailside privies when possible. Otherwise, bury your body waste in a trowel-deep hole well away from campsites and trails, and 200 feet from streams. Burn toilet paper and then cover the waste with soil and leaves.

Dogs

Dogs? Even where they are permitted—they are barred from trails in all national parks—they disturb the environment. They frighten animals and birds that you and others could have seen along the trail. And worse, they frighten hikers too. You may know your dog will not bite, but do others on the trail?

Leaf imprints in rock

Devil's club near Troublesome Creek (Hike 14)

So make it a rule. Don't take your dog unless it's necessary. Making it clear that the "necessity," in the eyes of others, is yours to defend.

Trailhead Parking

A sad warning about parking at trailheads: Leave nothing of value in your car. Anywhere. Seen or unseen. In the seat or in the trunk. And if you have an expensive radio, speakers, or CD gear, don't park at all.

And always look for loiterers when you arrive at a trailhead, particularly "hikers," or so they seem, who spend all of their time "just returning" from a hike or "getting ready" to start a hike. Note a license number if you can, jot down a description of those you see, and, if you return to damage or find the same "hikers" once again, report it to rangers or law enforcement officers. Sad. How sad.

Campgrounds

Campgrounds in this book are listed in the Appendix for each grouping of hikes. All of the campgrounds listed are operated by local, state, or federal agencies, which in many cases charge daily fees for the use of their facilities.

All of the camps include parking and tent areas, picnic tables, and fire pits. All have at least pit toilets. Water is available if indicated.

Space in the campgrounds, however, is not assured. Most of the camps are likely to be filled over weekends and holidays. Best opportunities occur midweek before or after school vacation periods. Reservations are available for some camps, as noted.

Many non-fee camps do not provide garbage services. In such camps take yours home. *Please,* take yours home.

And lest we forget: Remember how far sound carries in the woods. Keep your radio turned down, and remember that 10 P.M. is bedtime in every camp.

Backpacking

Many of the hikes here offer opportunities for short overnight backpack trips. Few, however, lead to spots that suggest prolonged vacations.

Backpack books (see Reading Suggestions) provide details on packs, cooking gear, sleeping bags, tents, and the like. Suffice it to say here that a short hike provides an opportunity to test your equipment, particularly if you have children along. For failure and even catastrophe will leave you only two miles or less from your car.

Enjoy (and Learn)

And then enjoy? Yes, most certainly. But, more important, beyond pleasure, look around you as you hike—see and try to understand.

While you drive forest roads to trailheads, for example, look closely and with purpose at what you see along the roads.

First, in the lower valleys, note how much of the summer green is brush and alders and how little of it is actually regrowing conifers, of the kind that once grew there.

Later, as your road climbs higher, pay attention to the

Camp Robber Creek (Hike 16)

clearcuts, new and old, and wonder at what you see. When you pass a sign that says "replanted" this year or that, or even if the clearcut is not signed, look closely at what commercial foresters call "reforestation." Fix the picture in your mind, and when you finally get to some small, ancient, uncut trail compare and wonder. Will those replanted forests stocked as advertised with two seedlings for every old tree cut down ever—*ever*—equal the uncut old forests you now enjoy? And next, would the logged forest you saw recover more certainly, and more grandly, if other methods—"practices" of logging, as they say—had been carried out?

And note, too, when you reach your trailhead how closely logging borders sometimes intrude on many of the sanctuaries here. Note how often you can see clearcuts through the trees and, in noting, wonder what impact those cleared areas will

have, or are having, on the "preserved" forest in which you walk.
From wind damage along the now-unprotected forest borders
over time? From changes in wildlife patterns caused by the
nearby removal of all the trees? On once-resident birds, rodents,
deer, or bear? On snowfall runoff in the spring? On the retention
of rainfall in the summer? On the mix of plants over time? Rest
assured as you make your guess that nobody else knows the an-
swers either.

And note often how suddenly everything changes around you
as you step beyond the signs that say "wilderness" or "park."
Sometimes as from night to day. You could almost ask: Who
needs the sign?

More important, as you wander past or through the forests
here, whether on state, federal, or private lands, remember: You
are the keeper of all these forests. What happens to all of them
depends on you.

You have a personal interest, and a right to have an interest,
in every clearcut, road, unlogged area, replanted site, wilderness, lake, waterfall, and river that you see. These forests are
yours to manage. Every one of them.

Your role in what you see on public forests—state or federal—is clear. You own them. It's your money being spent. Your
policies being carried out. You—yes, you—deserve the credit for
what is good, and you also deserve the blame for what is bad. For
you have received exactly what you asked for. And if you didn't
ask? Who else is there to blame?

And on private forests? On those huge, ugly, logged-off
blocks of railroad land. Trees—most of them—cut and shipped to
the Orient. You're responsible for those forests, too.

Private forests, throughout all of the nations of the Western
world, including those in Washington, are forests awarded to private owners to be held and used in trust for you. The public here
(in Europe, it was once the sovereign king) has, and always has
had, the right, the power, the obligation to demand that forests—
all forests—be managed in the public (in your, the sovereign's)
interest all the time.

And for all sorts of ancient and modern reasons. And all of
them so basic they are sometimes overlooked. Forests are necessary for all people—in the nation, in the world—for housing, recreation, stability of the soil, avalanche control, water retention,

weather, even air quality, along with the survival of birds, plants, and animals—just to begin a list.

Therefore, it's in your individual undisputed public interest—as the guardian of all forests in a democracy—to impose and enforce all necessary logging practices, controls, and restraints. And to impose them as you, the sovereign dispenser of all forest rights, think they should be in your (the public's) greatest interest.

Yes, enjoy what you find here. But, please, accept responsibility for everything you see. Demand for your children what you see yourself denied. Take steps to save every beauty that you see. Join others who seek what you seek. But, most important, act on your own behalf, speak for yourself and for your children and grandchildren, born and unborn, directly to those who represent you. And demand—yes, demand—that they respond personally to your wishes.

For again: They work for you. It's your money they spend. Your rules they make and enforce. Yours and yours alone. So take part. Insist. Demand. And, oh yes. Most certainly. Enjoy!

E. M. Sterling

A Note About Safety

Safety is an important concern in all outdoor activities. No guidebook can alert you to every hazard or anticipate the limitations of every reader. Therefore, the descriptions of roads, trails, routes, and natural features in this book are not representations that a particular place or excursion will be safe for your party. When you follow any of the routes described in this book, you assume responsibility for your own safety. Under normal conditions, such excursions require the usual attention to traffic, road and trail conditions, weather, terrain, the capabilities of your party, and other factors. Keeping informed on current conditions and exercising common sense are the keys to a safe, enjoyable outing.

The Mountaineers

Twin Falls State Park

Features: fine forest and two waterfalls
One way: about 1 mile
Elevation gain: 200 feet
Difficulty: moderate
Open: all year
Map: Green Trails 206

The falls you see here may never be what they might have been, but they're still worth hiking to.

Drive east on Snoqualmie Pass I-90 past North Bend, turn right at Edgewick Exit 34 and right again on Edgewick Road, and drive south to SE 159th Street. Turn left and drive to the end of the street in 1 mile.

The trail leaves the upriver end of the parking lot and wanders through rich forest for a half mile or more before turning uphill to a viewpoint and then beyond to spur trails leading to viewing platforms of the lower falls.

At the end of a mile, the path drops through boulders in a rain forest–like setting, kept moist by spray from the falls, to a bridge across the river above the lower falls.

Views up and down the river here. Hike on another 25 yards or so, up two short spurts of trail and a burst of steps, to the base of a great old Douglas fir for a head-on view of the upper falls.

The path continues up through more forest, along the edge of a clearcut, and down a powerline road to another parking area uphill to the right off I-90 Exit 38.

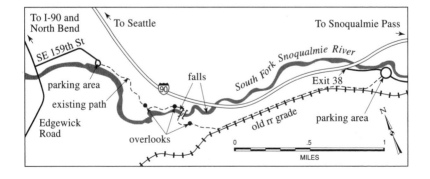

Twin Falls

Note as you view these falls that you may not be seeing them at their best, for a private power company diverts much of the water underground to power generators beneath state park land.

And note, too, that the public shares none of the $3 million generated by the company for the use of either the water or the land.

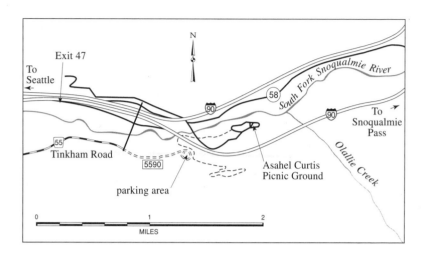

2 Asahel Curtis Nature Trail

Features: lush old-growth forest
One way: a short 1-mile loop
Elevation gain: slight
Difficulty: easy
Open: spring through fall
Map: Green Trails 207

The entrance sign says this grove of ancient trees contains about 140,000 board feet of lumber per acre. But ask yourself as you walk this trail: Does that total truly reflect the values here?

Drive east on Snoqualmie Pass I-90 and take Exit 47, turning right on Tinkham Road 55 at the end of the exit road. At a T intersection beyond the bridge over the Snoqualmie River, turn left on Road 5590 to a large parking area at the end of the road. Find the nature trail to the left of the trail to Annette Lake.

(You can also reach this trail from the Asahel Curtis Picnic Area across the two-lane freeway. Trails near the river there lead through more rich forest, crossing beneath the freeway before climbing up to the parking area [above] and nature loop.)

The path immediately enters a lush forest of old Douglas fir marred only by the constant howl of trucks and cars rushing up the nearby highway.

Discounting the noise, you can see the grandeur the photographer Asahel Curtis saw here. Notice how this beleaguered patch of trees, unassisted, has sustained its growth for centuries and survives still, despite the assaults of speeding humans.

Note how old tumbled giants are survived by towering giants, themselves awaiting their time to fall, all surrounded by other trees of every size and shape and age waiting for their future moment in the sun. An evolving forest here for sure, one that, if left alone, will always display a grandeur of ancient trees.

But wonder which in the end will win. The highway? Or Nature's trees? Also wonder: If traffic needs increase, will these trees fall too? Will the lumber extracted replace the value of what you see here now?

Humpback Creek, Asahel Curtis Nature Trail

Bathing Rock

3 Bathing Rocks

Features: natural water slides
One way: a long mile
Elevation gain: 500 feet
Difficulty: moderate
Open: summer
Map: Green Trails 207

Walk through old forest near a pretty creek to a basking place near eroded chutes in polished rock where children and adults often shout and play.

Drive east on Snoqualmie Pass I-90, turn off at Exit 47, and cross left over the freeway and then right beyond the westbound entrance on Denny Creek Road 58. In about 2.5 miles pass Denny Creek Campground, turning left onto a road that crosses the river, passes some private homes, and ends at a large parking lot.

Take the Melakwa Lake Trail off the upper end of the parking loop.

The path starts above Denny Creek and then drops across a bridge before climbing beneath the freeway perched on stilts far above the trail, a European fashion that does little damage to the forest. In fact, except for the pops of vehicles crossing highway expansion joints, you may not hear the traffic here at all. An example, certainly, of what engineers can do when they want to avoid destruction of a mountainside in the construction of a freeway.

The trail levels off slightly as it continues to the Alpine Lakes Wilderness through more rich forest filled with ferns, berries, and flowers in their season.

Way paths lead to views down on some rock ledges before the trail crosses a log bridge over the creek to the popular rock water slides. The path straight ahead also leads to the water's edge but, when the stream is high, not to the other side.

The creek here, warmed by the sun and rocks, permits sliding all summer long in the tumbling water chutes with a lot of places to picnic and watch from shoreside slabs.

And plan on a lot of activity on warm weekends. You won't believe the cross-section of young and old, fat and thin, you'll find hiking here to join children playing in the slippery chutes.

Hike upward beyond the crossing for another half mile to views of Keekwulee Falls and up another bunch of switchbacks more to Snowshoe Falls.

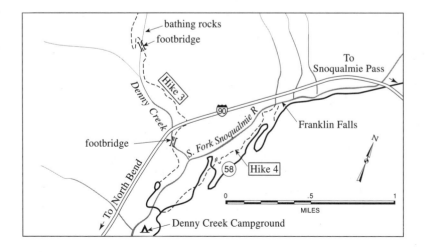

4 Franklin Falls

Features: waterfall
One way: ¼ mile or longer
Elevation gain: slight
Difficulty: moderate
Open: whenever the road is free of snow
Map: Green Trails 207

Take a short walk to what may be one of the most popular and accessible public waterfalls in Mount Baker–Snoqualmie National Forest. And then wonder if the water that plunges over it ought to be diverted to a private power plant.

Drive east on Snoqualmie Pass I-90, turn off at Exit 47, and cross left over the freeway and then right beyond the westbound entrance to Denny Creek Road 58 (see map on page 21).

For the shortest walk drive a mile beyond Denny Creek Campground to a small parking area at the end of the third sharp switchback in the road. Find the trail off the road to the left.

Longer trails start at the bridge over Denny Creek off the access road to the Melakwa Lake Trail (see Hike 3, Bathing Rocks, for directions) or up the road to the second sharp switchback to a section of the Wagon Road Trail.

The shortest path drops sharply to the base of the falls, which plunges 70 feet over a cliff. In summer, rest awhile on a gravel bar at the base of the falls along (on weekends) with hordes of others.

Note while you are there how the freeway high above you impinges on the scene, destroying any sense of "forest" now. And then wonder what further impact a diversion of much of the river's water around the falls to a power plant would have.

A private developer seeks to dam the river above the falls and divert water through pipes, buried near the road, to a power-house on public land downstream below the campground.

The Forest Service has already decided that diversion of the river and construction of the powerhouse are not precluded by any of its regulations, although the agency says it will still consider the impact of the project on wildlife, fish, scenic values, and public use.

It is unlikely, however, that the Forest Service or any other local, state, or federal agency will conduct any public hearings either on the merit of the necessity for the dam or on the impact of any diversion on the falls.

The developer has already obtained a preliminary permit and hopes for a permanent go-ahead from the Federal Energy Regulatory Commission (FERC).

If you wish to comment on the proposal while there's still time (once the FERC makes up its mind, all other issues may be moot), write a letter to the Supervisor, Mount Baker–Snoqualmie National Forest, 21905 64th Avenue West, Mountlake Terrace, WA 98043. As you write, remember that we, who own the falls and water, will get nothing for any recreation losses we may suffer.

Remember: It's public land and public money and ought to be a public choice.

Franklin Falls

5 Snow Lake

Features: high mountain lake
One way: 3½ miles
Elevation gain: 1,700 feet
Difficulty: moderate to steep
Open: midsummer
Map: Green Trails 207

You can meet twenty to sixty people walking this trail with you on a weekday, even more on weekends. Yet the lake, at 4,016 feet, still remains one of the most beautiful places you can hike to so close to Seattle.

Drive east on Snoqualmie Pass I-90 to Snoqualmie Pass, turning off at Exit 52 and then left at the end of the exit road onto Alpental Road. Drive underneath the freeway and follow Alpental Road to its end in 1.5 miles in a parking area near a ski resort.

The trail starts up sharply off the upper right-hand corner of the lot. It quickly enters a forest of handsome ancient mountain hemlocks, crosses an avalanche area strewn with huge trees mowed down by plunging snow, passes a small waterfall, and crosses still more rockfalls and avalanche chutes.

At 1½ miles the trail, strewn each fall with fir cone cores

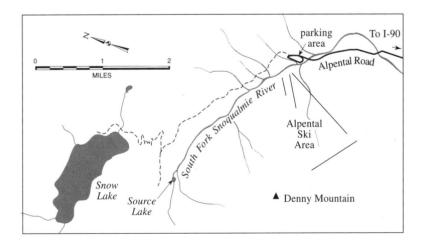

Snow Lake

stripped clean by chipmunks and Douglas squirrels, reaches a junction (a ½-mile trail left leads to a view down on Source Lake) and then starts switchbacking up a ridge. Higher and higher views back over the valley and Alpine Village as you climb. (Take care not to kick rocks downhill as you hike here: others may be just below you.)

After some nine switchbacks the path enters the Alpine Lakes Wilderness and makes one last long traverse to the top of a ridge at 4,800 feet before starting down to the lake you see below.

The well-worn path, in heather meadows now, drops down four switchbacks across roots and rocks to spur paths leading to identified camping spots and to the cabin site you saw from the top of the ridge.

Find your own viewing spot amid the meadows, creeks, and tarns, avoiding the many areas marked with signs, some posted for 20 years, or blocked off by newer colored tapes put up to protect "restoration" areas from further overuse.

Some 17,000 people made their way here in 1992. The yearly hordes so far have not destroyed the snow-laden peaks across the lake, but they have most certainly worn the ground cover bare in all of the most popular viewing spots, although—to give the warning signs their due—not as extensively as the damage might have been, as new growing trees around the cabin now attest.

The main path continues past a junction with a trail that goes over a ridge to the middle fork of the Snoqualmie and then 2 miles to Gem Lake and another 2 miles to Lower Wildcat Lake.

6   Mirror and Cottonwood Lakes

Features: two lakes on one trail
One way: 1¼ miles
Elevation gain: 600 feet
Difficulty: moderate to steep
Open: summer
Map: Green Trails 207

Two mountain lakes in a little over a mile, both set in rich old forest yet each of them different—and worthy of a visit.

Drive east on Snoqualmie Pass I-90 and turn off at Exit 62, just beyond Lake Keechelus and about 10 miles east from the top of Snoqualmie Pass.

Turn right onto Road 54, cross the Yakima River, and turn right again on Road 5480 in about 0.5 mile. Follow the road past Lost Lake. At a fork beyond the lake turn right. Pause at the next left at the base of a steep, sometimes rough uphill spur and judge whether you should drive on or park and walk the last half-mile to the trailhead.

The path starts out in a brushy clearcut but, in 100 yards or less, enters an old forest, following old blazes and crossing a

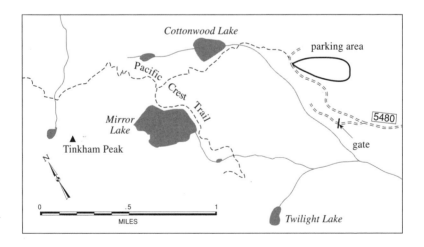

Mirror Lake and Tinkham Peak

creek before climbing sharply (but shortly) to Cottonwood Lake at 3,900 feet, the shallower of the two. Stop here for sure before climbing higher (on switchbacks now) above Cottonwood Lake through a saddle to a heather meadow, a small tarn, the Pacific Crest Trail, and, almost immediately to the left, Mirror Lake at 4,200 feet in its forest basin.

The trail continues above the lake to the far end with a more open area in which to camp. Loiter here for sure.

7   Big Tree Nature Trail

Features: beautiful forest
One way: ½-mile loop
Elevation gain: none
Difficulty: easy
Open: summer
Map: Green Trails 208

No matter how long or far you've tramped in the Northwest mountains, you'll not find a finer example of an old-growth forest at this elevation (2,500 feet) anywhere. Best early in the morning or on a summer evening.

Drive east on Snoqualmie Pass I-90 over Snoqualmie Pass, turning off at Exit 62 then left over the freeway to follow Road 49 to the entrance of Kachess Campground in about 5 miles.

Once through the entry station, turn right at a T intersection and find the small parking area on the right side of the road. The trail is across the road.

Truthfully, there's not much to be said about this forest loop, for how can you describe a grand cathedral, anywhere. You can feel its grandeur, yes, but it goes far beyond a mundane list of details and words.

It's awesome, certainly. As in a great cathedral, you feel here, too, that you intrude—that you must walk softly here and hushed.

There are towering trees, most certainly: ancient Douglas fir,

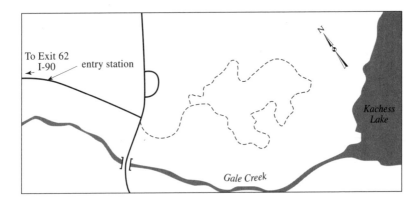

Big Tree Nature Trail

hemlock, and cedar trees. Deadfalls, new growth, berries, ferns, devil's club, vine maples, flowers (different ones in different seasons), all tumbled together (or so it seems) in a continuing, still-evolving forest that has already ruled here century after century. A constant mix of plants and animals in a still-constant state of growth and death.

Yet it's still a place of separate things. So take your flower and bird books with you and give each separate thing its name. Read all the signs, sit on all the benches, and listen to the birds and wind. Notice where the forest was blown down here, burned there, sent up new seedling trees atop every rotting log.

Remembering the total place as a cathedral built by Nature—just for you.

8   Little Kachess Lake

Features: changing forest and lake
One way: 1 mile or more
Elevation gain: 250 feet
Difficulty: easy to steep (wheelchair section)
Open: summer
Maps: Green Trails 208; campground brochure

First, an introduction to the forest here on an easy, gravel trail. Then, a rougher illustration of an old-fashioned trail of rocks and roots that struggles up and down above the lake to destinations miles to the north.

Drive east on Snoqualmie Pass I-90 over Snoqualmie Pass, turning off at Exit 62 and turning left over the freeway to follow Road 49 to the entrance of Kachess Campground in about 5 miles.

Beyond the entry station turn left at the T intersection and follow the campground road to the boat launch area, continuing left again around a parking loop to a spur right that leads to the trailhead parking area.

From the parking area take the trail past a display to a log bridge over Box Canyon Creek in less than 100 yards. Follow the

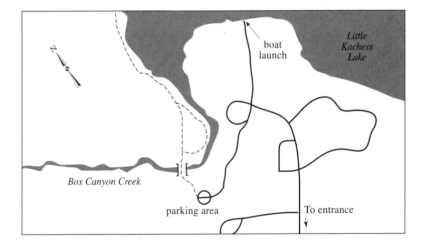

Little Kachess

barrier-free trail to the right to points overlooking the lake with displays that explain the full spectrum of nature here.

At the end of the loop, the paved path climbs to a bluff overlook with the fullest view of the lake and mountains across the way.

For a true sense of the ruggedness of these shores, proceed north beyond the end of the paved loop to the original lake trail. Here, the path, sometimes level and sometimes steep, skirts cliffs and bluffs or passes through old forest, seldom reaching the water's edge.

Go as far as the spirit moves you. In a little more than 4½ miles, at the upper end of the lake, the trail reaches a junction with the Mineral Creek Trail, which leads into the Alpine Lakes Wilderness.

Cooper Lake

9   Cooper River Trail

Features: forest and wild river
One way: 3¼ miles from beginning to end
Elevation gain: 400 feet
Difficulty: moderate to steep
Open: summer
Map: Green Trails 208

Two choices here: Walk generally downhill from Cooper Lake at 2,800 feet, or walk a shorter distance slightly uphill on the lower trail to view the pools not far from Salmon la Sac Campground at 2,400 feet.

From Snoqualmie Pass I-90 turn off either at Exit 80 over the freeway to Bullfrog Road or at Exit 84 over the freeway to

Cle Elum, driving in both instances to Highway 903, Roslyn, and beyond.

To hike *down* the river trail, drive about 18 miles north of Cle Elum on Road 903, turning left on Road 46 to cross the Cle Elum River and in 4.7 miles right on Spur Road 113. Find the trailhead downhill to the right in 0.2 mile, just beyond the bridge over the Cooper River.

To hike *up* the river trail from Salmon la Sac Campground, drive about 19 miles from Cle Elum to the end of paved Road 903. Take the spur road to the right as you enter the campground, and find the trailhead in another 0.5 mile at the end of the road.

The trail *down* the river from Cooper Lake drops near the river through great old Douglas firs and hemlock to rock-slab views and fishing holes within a quarter mile. The path then passes through more lush forest and by more rock ledges, pools, and rapids before climbing away from the river to a cedar-guarded stream crossing—and a resting bench.

The trail now climbs up and down, sometimes out of earshot of the river, before dropping sharply back to spectacular views into a gorge of more torrents, pools, and rapids before finally reaching river level once again.

From the Salmon la Sac trailhead, walk *upstream* past rapids, cliffs, and pools, picking the best place to stop, look, and listen to the stream. Walk about ¼ mile farther up the trail, climbing about 200 feet, for a fuller vista down on the river.

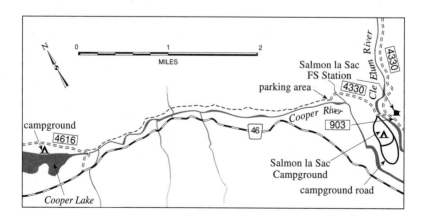

10 Tucquala Meadows

Features: flower meadow
One way: as far as you like
Elevation gain: none
Difficulty: wet
Open: Memorial Day or later
Map: Green Trails 176

Too many flowers here to even attempt to identify—each at its own time and in its own season. But some of almost everything at this elevation (3,400 feet) between the melting snows of spring and fall.

From Snoqualmie Pass I-90 take either Exit 80 over the freeway to Bullfrog Road or Exit 84 over the freeway to Cle Elum, driving in both instances to Highway 903, Roslyn, and beyond.

Drive to the end of paved Highway 903 in 19 miles from Cle Elum, bearing right up gravel Road 4330 at a point where the paved road turns left to cross the river.

In another 10 miles find the meadow to the left just beyond Tucquala (Fish) Lake across from a guard station and Fish Lake Campground. (The meadow and trail-end of this sometimes rough road are blocked every spring by high water over the road at Scatter Creek. Check with the Cle Elum District Ranger Station about conditions before Memorial Day for sure.)

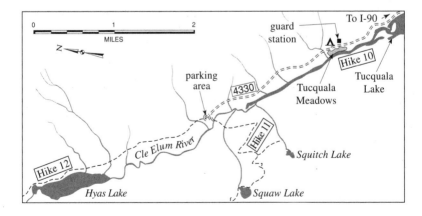

Cathedral Rock from Tucquala Meadows

The meadow extends from the road to the Cle Elum River and from the primitive camp at the south to forest at the north.

There are no trails in this meadow, nor should there be. This meadow is strictly for flowers, wild, unnamed, and unmarked, to be found wherever they grow in whatever time of summer you visit there.

Early in the spring, fields of blue-eyed grass are followed by larger fields of shooting stars. Later, columbines and tiger lilies, cotton grass and bog orchids, elephant head and chocolate lilies (if you're there on time). And those only start the list.

Bring rubber boots of some kind, for the meadows are soggy all summer long. Carry bug lotion if there is no wind. Take your flower book and camera for sure, and then wander where you will.

Leave all the flowers where you find them, naturally. If everyone who came this way took a flower home, there soon would be none left.

And, oh yes, explore the river's edge, watch for deer in the meadow, and sometimes, if you are lucky, glimpse across the stream—a bear.

11 Squaw Lake

Features: lake and vistas
One way: 2 miles
Elevation gain: 1,450 feet
Difficulty: moderate to steep
Open: summer
Map: Green Trails 176

Big peaks and bigger lakes can't overawe this alpine gem. Walk slightly more than 2 miles from a beautiful valley to an equally beautiful lake surrounded by its own worthwhile peaks.

From Snoqualmie Pass I-90 turn off either at Exit 80 over the freeway to Bullfrog Road or at Exit 84 over the freeway to Cle Elum, driving in both instances to Highway 903, Roslyn, and beyond.

Drive to the end of paved Highway 903 in 19 miles, bearing right up gravel Road 4330 at a point where the paved road turns left to cross the Cle Elum River. Find the trailhead in about 13 miles (almost at the end of Road 4330) off a short spur road to the left. (See map on page 34.)

From the parking area, the trail crosses a bridge over the Cle Elum River into old forest in the Alpine Lakes Wilderness and then starts a 1,000-foot climb up long switchbacks to the top of a ridge and a junction with a trail down Trail Creek.

Turn right toward Cathedral Rock and climb more gradually now along the side of a ridge (views here over the valley) to the wooded, subalpine lake tucked in heather at 4,850 feet at the base of a rocky cliff. Piles of snow here last into the summer.

A worthy place to stop, with boulders to rest and lunch on. However, if the spirit moves you (and it well may not), walk on north toward Cathedral Rock into a series of meadows, rock outcrops, and patches of forest before turning back.

Squaw Lake

12 Hyas Lake

Features: lake below Cathedral Rock
One way: 2 miles or less
Elevation gain: slight
Difficulty: easy
Open: summer
Map: Green Trails 176

One of the easiest and most spectacular trips in this entire book.

From Snoqualmie Pass I-90 turn off either at Exit 80 over the freeway to Bullfrog Road or at Exit 84 over the freeway to Cle Elum, driving in both instances to Highway 903, Roslyn, and beyond.

Drive to the end of Highway 903 in about 19 miles, bearing right up gravel Road 4330 at a point where the paved road turns left to cross the Cle Elum River. Find the trailhead off the end of a parking area at the end of Road 4330 in about 13 miles. (See map on page 34.)

The path wanders through an old-growth forest and along the edge of occasional meadows to a pretty lake nested below Cathedral Rock and Mount Daniel at 3,550 feet. Camp spots in timber just before the trail reaches the lake; other camp spots along the 1-mile lake.

The trail continues on to Little Hyas Lake in ¼ mile and on to Deception Pass at 4,500 feet in another 2½ miles. Views down on the lakes and up at the mountains from open slopes to the pass.

Much of the heavy wear on the trails here dates back to when the Pacific Crest Trail passed this way. Now the Crest Trail climbs across the ridge on the other side of the lakes. You may spot hikers there.

Note: At the beginning of this trail, as it climbs slightly from the parking lot, watch for an ant (yes, ant) "highway" at your feet alongside the trail. And as you start to crest this slight rise, look to your right for a huge ant hill that may still be there. If it is, walk to it and listen to the hum of a hard-working metropolis of ants. And note again the steady traffic on the much-traveled but well-maintained ant freeway beside the trail.

Hyas Lake

13 Wallace Falls

Features: waterfall
One way: 2 miles or more
Elevation gain: up to 1,100 feet
Difficulty: moderate to steep
Open: all year
Map: Green Trails 142

You can glimpse this waterfall high in the mountains to the left of Stevens Pass Highway 2 as you drive to Gold Bar. But with a little effort, you can feel its cold spray, too. One of the most popular, accessible, and spectacular waterfalls in the region.

Drive east on the Stevens Pass Highway 2 through Monroe to Gold Bar, following signs to the left 2 miles to Wallace Falls State Park. The trail to the falls is clearly marked at the end of the limited parking area, which may be filled on summer weekends.

The path starts out (at 600 feet) below an unexciting powerline and turns shortly into a dense, second-growth forest before reaching a fork in another 100 yards.

By continuing left on the railroad grade, it's 2 miles on a still slow-climbing and uneventful path to where the two trails join again. Or, by dropping downhill to the right, it's a shorter but

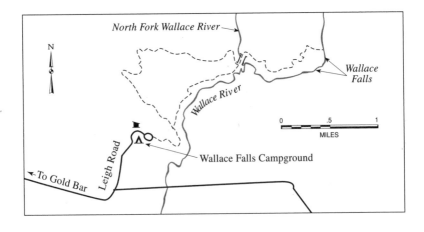

North Fork Wallace River

Wallace Falls

Wallace River

N

0   .5   1
MILES

Leigh Road

To Gold Bar

Wallace Falls Campground

Wallace Falls

steeper mile, crossing a wooden bridge and then climbing generally through a dense forest of hemlock and Douglas fir amid alders and vine maples, ferns, and forest wild flowers in season.

From the juncture of both trails, walk another ¼ mile to a
picnic shelter (870 feet) and views up at the falls. Or climb ahead
to a middle viewpoint (1,120 feet), or still farther to a view of the
valley (1,400 feet), or still farther in 3 miles (1,700 feet) to an
explosive vista of everything: down on the falls, out over the
valley, across at the mountains on the other side, and out on the
string of villages along the river. Each and every point is worth
the effort.

14 Troublesome Creek

Features: grand forest plus a wild stream
One way: ½-mile loop
Elevation gain: slight
Difficulty: moderate
Open: summer
Map: Green Trails 143

What was once an old miners' trail is now a busy and pretty interpretive trail along and around a tumbling, noisy creek.

Drive east on Stevens Pass Highway 2 through Gold Bar, turning left in about 8 miles toward Index on North Fork Road 63. In about 11 miles turn right into the Troublesome Creek Campground entrance. Take a stub road immediately to the left, and park near a footbridge over Troublesome Creek. Don't cross the footbridge. Find your path up the left side of the creek. (You'll return to the far side of the bridge at the end of your walk.)

The path dips under the highway bridge and proceeds upstream above a very noisy creek through a towering old forest of Douglas fir and cedar trees.

The path climbs to a viewpoint over a roaring gorge where water races one way and then turns and plunges another, all the while sculpting bowls and sweeping curves in shoreside rock.

Beyond the view and resting point, the trail wanders through

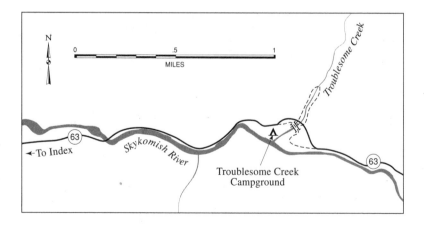

Troublesome Creek

a forest of monstrous boulders to a bridge where the stream again displays the essence of its violence. An undeveloped upriver path on the far side of the bridge crosses inviting slabs and eroded folds of rock near an ancient cedar still clinging to its perch on the very edges of the stream.

The main path turns right on the far side of the bridge to climb past more old giants surrounded by fallen, rotting snags of failed competitors, more forest flowers, plus the sounds of birds, squirrels, and chipmunks above the noise of the creek.

At the base of a giant Douglas fir on this part of the trail, pause for a moment on a bench and rejoice that such forests can still be seen, heard, smelled, touched, and, if huckleberries are in fruit, tasted, too.

When you see the road, follow switchbacks down to the river, crossing beneath the road and over the wooden bridge back to your car.

15 Barclay Lake

Features: forest and lake
One way: 1½ miles
Elevation gain: 100 feet
Difficulty: moderate
Open: summer
Map: Green Trails 143

Walk out of a recovering clearcut into a rich forest and then on to a lake at 2,300 feet with places to sit and dream in the shadow of spectacular Baring Mountain.

Drive east on Stevens Pass Highway 2 from Monroe through Gold Bar, past the Index junction, and in another 6 miles to the village of Baring, turning left across the railroad tracks as you reach the store on the right. Across the railroad tracks proceed straight ahead, bearing left on Road 6024 at the edge of town. Trailhead at the end of the road in about 4.5 miles.

The trail starts up an old fireline, turning right to the unmarked main trail in about ¼ mile. The path then enters a forest that appears to be in a state of terminal collapse. Yet everywhere around you: a classic example of an old-growth forest, evolving still with broken snags filled with woodpecker holes, snarls of

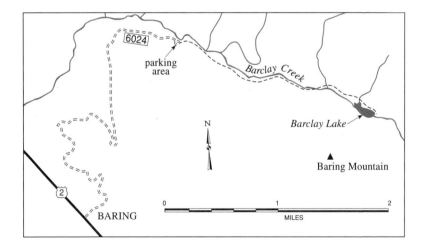

Barclay Lake below Baring Mountain

fallen rotting trees, and a ground littered with what seems like wasted debris. But all of it below a forest of old-growth giants towering above younger trees waiting in the shade for their time and place in the sun and towering in turn over new seedlings on the mossy forest floor.

And note also the forest floor: held intact by both old and living roots, protected by a sponge of duff and moss, awash with huckleberries, salmonberries, fireweed, and flowers of the shade.

The trail crosses Barclay Creek shortly before reaching the lake below the towering walls of Baring Mountain. The path proceeds the full length of the shore with your choice of camp, picnic, and viewing spots. Busy on weekends, however.

16 Lake Dorothy

Features: large mountain lake
One way: 2 miles
Elevation gain: 800 feet
Difficulty: moderate to steep
Open: summer
Map: Green Trails 175

The biggest alpine lake and one of the most beautiful on the west side of the Cascade Crest—with waterfalls en route.

Drive east on Stevens Pass Highway 2 about 11 miles beyond Index, turning right, just before you reach the tunnel west of Skykomish, to the old Cascade Highway and Money Creek Campground. In a little more than a mile, turn right again onto Miller River Road 6412 and drive to trailhead parking at the end.

Take at least two snacks on this walk. Eat the first at the footbridge over Camp Robber Creek (water ouzels but no camp robbers here). Save the rest for the final steep pitch to the log-jammed outlet of the lake at 3,000 feet.

The trail continues along the east side of the 2-mile-long, island-dotted lake, turning westward across the marshy far end before climbing on to more distant Bear, Deer, and Snoqualmie lakes.

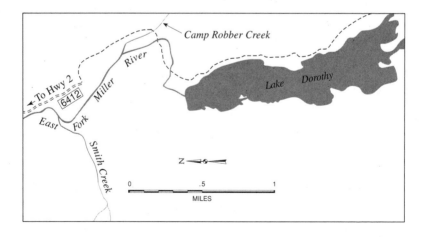

Lake Dorothy

Trail below Evergreen Lookout after a September snowstorm

 # 17 Evergreen Lookout

Features: spectacular vistas and high meadow
One way: 1½ miles
Elevation gain: 1,300 feet
Difficulty: steep to very steep
Open: midsummer
Map: Green Trails 143
Note: Check road access before leaving

Climb to high meadows and one of the most spectacular clear-day views of this section of the Cascades.

Drive east on Stevens Pass Highway 2 from Everett or Monroe to Skykomish, turning north on Beckler River Road 65 and driving about 12.5 miles to Jack Pass and Road 6550/54, to the right. Follow 6554 as it winds up across Evergreen Creek and then zigzags back to the south over more slopes, logged after a 1967 fire, before switchbacking up to the trailhead at 4,300 feet in more than 8 miles. Big views even from the road.

The trail takes off at the end of the spur road, switchbacks up a logged area and partially burned ridge, traverses an unburned slope, and then bursts suddenly in the last ½ mile into open, flower-filled meadows.

The lookout, perched on the ground at 5,585 feet, provides a 360-degree view of Glacier Peak, Mount Rainier, and the Monte Cristo peaks. Wander a little way down the ridge east of the lookout on an abandoned trail to a lunch spot with your own private view. Bring water.

A note of concern: Thirty years ago hikers had to climb 6 miles and more over virgin slopes to reach this lookout. After the fire and logging, the distance dropped to 1½ miles. As this book was being written, some would increase the distance again— over the blocked logging road or up a new steep trail—because the road was washed out by floods and storms. This poses several questions: Should the public's investment in this forest road be abandoned due to such damage just because the logging's done? Did the public intend to spend its money to build this road solely to subsidize a logging operation? Would the road have been repaired for use by loggers? And should anyone have to pretend that a logging road is truly like a trail? Or be forced to pay for some new makeshift trail that would probably cost as much as a road repair?

Consider these matters if you learn the road is to be, or has been, abandoned, and let the Supervisor of Mount Baker–Snoqualmie National Forest know what you think.

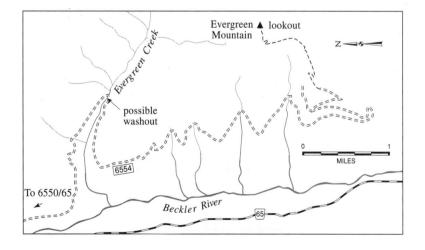

18   Tonga Ridge

Features: forest, meadows, vistas
One way: 2 miles, more or less
Elevation gain: up to 300 feet
Difficulty: moderate
Open: summer
Maps: Green Trails 175, 176

In less than 2 miles, climb a forested ridge to grass meadows at 4,600 to 4,800 feet along Tonga Ridge with views of Glacier Peak south through the glaciers of Mount Hinman. Lots of huckleberries in the fall.

Drive east on Stevens Pass Highway 2 from Everett or Monroe to Skykomish, turning south (right) on Foss River Road 68, about 0.5 mile east of the Skykomish District Ranger Station. In 3.7 miles turn left uphill on Road 6830, driving another 6.8 miles to Spur Road 310 uphill to the right. Trailhead at the end of the spur road in less than 1.5 miles.

(Continue on Road 6830 to views of the valley and mountains to the north. Take your forest map to identify all the peaks.)

The trail, off the end of a parking area, starts out on the edge of a firelane of an old clearcut and shortly climbs into a changing forest of silver fir, hemlock, and alpine fir that opens onto mead-

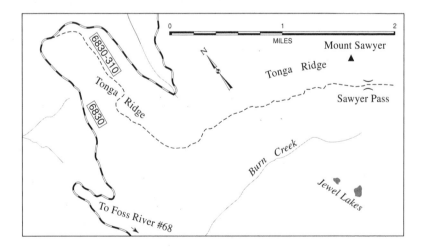

Tonga Ridge Trail

ows in about 1½ miles. Watch for a spur trail to the left here up to the first of several viewpoints on the ridge.

The main trail drops slightly, but climbs again to more open meadows on the south slope of the ridge. Again, take spur trails to the ridgetop for the best in vistas.

Ample places to pause and enjoy amid lots of lupine and hummingbirds anxious to check out anything that's red.

19 Trout Lake

Features: lake, forest, rockfalls
One way: 1½ miles
Elevation gain: 400 feet
Difficulty: moderate
Open: summer
Map: Green Trails 175

Hike through groves of grand old Douglas fir, past huge boulders that have tumbled from cliffs above you, over an avalanche of rocks to an interesting—and pleasant—mountain lake at 2,000-plus feet.

Drive east on Stevens Pass Highway 2 past Skykomish, turning south (right) on Foss River Road 68 about 0.5 mile east of the Skykomish District Ranger Station. Follow Road 68 as it jogs to the left in about 5 miles and continues to trailhead parking at the end of the road.

The heavily used trail starts at the end of the parking area and enters the Alpine Lakes Wilderness in 100 yards or so, crossing a gravel bar to a log bridge over the Foss River in about ½ mile.

The trail travels through groves of hemlock and Douglas fir and past an array of giant boulders, which over centuries have

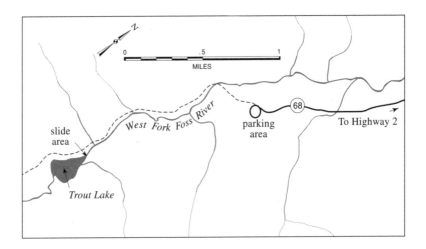

tumbled off the pinnacles that rim the valley and hint at rockfall yet to come.

In about 1 mile the path pauses at a giant Douglas fir and then climbs to views back on it as it towers alone: king of the forest here. As the trail turns back into the forest, note pipes exposed across the trail—remnants of a failed mining operation here.

The path drops to the river again and crosses a fresh avalanche of rock before reaching the lake. This massive mound of rock plunged more than 1,000 feet across the original trail off the cliffs of Malachite Peak during a thunderstorm on a busy Saturday in August 1991 while hikers camped at the lake nearby.

The rock dammed the Foss River outlet, raised the lake 7 feet, and swamped sections of the trail, leaving trees now standing in the water, dead, along the upper shore.

Camp and resting spots beyond the rockfall. The trail continues along the lake before climbing almost 2,000 feet more to still other lakes.

Trout Lake

20 Evans Lake

Features: small and pleasant mountain lake
One way: ½ mile
Elevation gain: slight
Difficulty: easy
Open: summer
Map: Green Trails 175

A short path through rich forest leads to a pretty, wooded lake just inside the Alpine Lakes Wilderness.

Drive east on Stevens Pass Highway 2 past Skykomish, turning south (right) on Foss River Road 68 about 0.5 mile east of the Skykomish District Ranger Station. In about 5 miles, as Road 68 jogs to the left to Trout Lake, continue ahead on Road 6840 (views over the valley as you climb), turning right on Road 6846 in about 4 miles and driving another 2.5 miles to the trailhead (keep left at the 2-mile marker). The trail is signed uphill on the right across from a parking area just before the road crosses the bridge over the Evans Lake outlet creek.

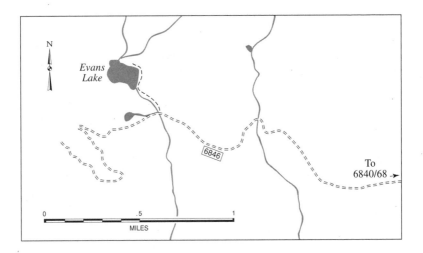

Evans Lake

The path climbs gently through heather along the creek in open, lush forest, arriving suddenly at the lake. The path continues around the lake to the right past a couple of camp spots at the upper end.

A peaceful place. What's more to say?

21 Iron Goat Trail

Features: railroad history and views
One way: 2 miles or more
Elevation gain: about 200 feet
Difficulty: moderate to easy (some wheelchair access)
Open: summer
Map: Ask for brochure at the Forest Service ranger station in
Skykomish

Walk an easy wheelchair trail through railroad history or
climb spur trails to a hiker-only path on a higher section of the
old Great Northern railroad grade with more history still.

(First phase of construction scheduled for completion in Oc-
tober 1993.)

Drive east on Stevens Pass Highway 2 through Skykomish,
turning north at Milepost 55 onto paved but unsigned Road 67.
(If you miss that turn continue another 3.5 miles toward Scenic,
turning left onto the other end of the same Road 67.) Continue
from either end of Road 67 to Road 6710, uphill to the north, finding the trailhead in about 1.5 miles. Parking area along the road.
(See map on page 58.)

The well-developed wheelchair path starts through an alder
grove filled with berry bushes and ferns and continues little
more than a mile down the lower section of the railway right-of-
way past viewpoints to a tunnel portal at a washed out creek.
(Footpaths on this lower stretch of trail will eventually drop to
Scenic on Highway 2.)

A hiker trail leads uphill in the first ½ mile of the lower trail
to a higher switchback level on the old railroad bed, which includes other collapsed tunnels and snowsheds. A second trail
drops down to form a 1½-mile loop. Or continue east on the upper level to a viewpoint beyond a collapsed flume in about 2
miles, returning to the trailhead in a total of 5½ miles.

The upper trail will eventually end near the top of Stevens
Pass at the old townsite of Wellington, destroyed along with a passenger train in an avalanche in which 96 passengers were killed.

These trails are all within the Stevens Pass Historic District,
which extends over Stevens Pass and includes Deception Creek

(see Hike 22, Deception Falls), a future Wellington townsite display, and the Bygone Byways rail and highway trail (see Hike 26, Bygone Byways).

The Great Northern Railway, which featured a mountain goat in its corporate emblem, built this line from Chicago to Seattle between 1897 and 1900 and abandoned it in 1929 after completing the present 8-mile tunnel with an entrance near Scenic, which is still used by Burlington Northern Railroad, Great Northern's corporate inheritor.

Wall No. 1 (the waterfall wall) was part of a former snowshed.

22 Deception Falls

Features: wild waterfalls in rich forest
One way: ¾-mile loop
Elevation gain: less than 200 feet
Difficulty: easy to moderate (wheelchair access)
Open: spring to fall
Map: Green Trails 176

Come face to face with a raging torrent and then walk through a peaceful forest to lesser tumults on a creek fed by a half-dozen or more lakes in the Alpine Lakes Wilderness.

Drive east on Stevens Pass Highway 2 about 8 miles beyond Skykomish to a signed parking area on the north (left) side of the highway.

The path starts to the left of a picnic shelter, dropping downhill to the right on a wheelchair portion of the path that leads across a bridge over the creek to a platform beneath the highway with a spectacular and noisy head-on view of the falls only feet away.

Return to the loop trail and drop to the right downhill across a log bridge to a quieter part of the creek in ancient, rain forest–like groves and then on to an overlook of another falls that tumbles

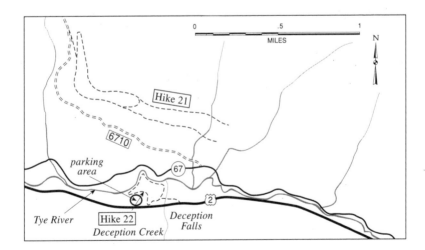

Deception Falls with highway and footbridge

into a pretty pool filled with rainbows if the sun's just right.

The path passes still more pools and then another small falls, sometimes snagged with logs thrown up on rocks during high water in the spring, reaching a more subdued section of stream where falls turn into rapids before climbing back to picnic shelter.

Note as you climb toward the highway the great stumps of trees logged by hand by men who stood on springboards, jammed into the notches in stumps, to hand-saw the tree.

Display boards describe natural features along the way.

The falls development is within the Stevens Pass Historic District.

Hope Lake

23 Hope Lake

Features: alpine lake and meadows
One way: about 1½ miles
Elevation gain: 1,300 feet
Difficulty: steep to very steep
Open: midsummer
Map: Green Trails 176

You don't have to walk far but you do have to climb persistently to a pretty little mountain lake tucked into the very crest of the Cascades at 4,400 feet.

Drive 12 miles east of Skykomish on Stevens Pass Highway 2, turning right onto Road 6095 a little more than 1 mile beyond the railroad overpass at Scenic and just before the highway widens to four lanes on a sharp highway turn. On Road 6095 turn right in 0.6 mile onto Spur Road 110. Continue straight ahead at the next junction in 0.8 mile, turning right in 1.2 miles onto Spur Road 112. Road 112 climbs steeply 1.3 miles to the trailhead at 3,000 feet.

The path, much of it built and maintained by The Mountaineers Singles, starts out in forest and then settles down to a steady climb above Tunnel Creek, reaching a saddle and the small lake (in Chelan County) on the Pacific Crest Trail at 4,400 feet.

But don't hurry away. If you've got time—and you should plan to take it—walk either north or south (or both) on the Crest Trail, exploring other meadows and heathered tarns.

The trail northerly toward Stevens Pass climbs over the divide to Mig Lake (4,600 feet in King County) in about ¾ mile. The path to the south climbs past unnamed tarns before climbing higher on the ridge.

And, finally, after soaking up all vistas right and left, promise to return again.

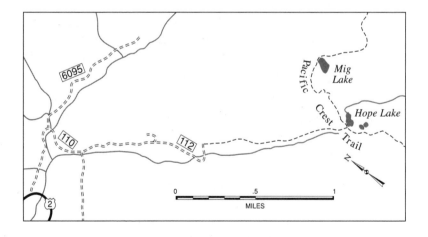

24 Skyline Lake and Grace Lakes

Features: small alpine lakes
One way: 1½–2 miles or more
Elevation gain: 750–1,100 feet
Difficulty: steep
Open: midsummer
Map: Green Trails 176 (shows lakes only)

"Roads" both north and south of Stevens Pass lead to surprising alpine lakes tucked in heather meadows that make the
uphill efforts worth the struggle.

Drive east on Stevens Pass Highway 2 to Stevens Pass, some
56 miles from Everett, 42 miles from Monroe.

To reach Skyline Lake, park on the north side of the highway
near a spur road that leads uphill off the west end of the large
parking area. (Do not park on the spur road that leads through a
residential area.)

To reach Grace Lakes from Seattle, turn right into the first
ski area parking lot as you approach the pass, driving to the
west end of the upper lot. If the lot is gated, park near the gate.

Find the steep, rutted jeep path to Skyline Lake (1½ miles
and up 750 feet) off the end of the parking lot spur road as it
starts uphill beneath a powerline. The one-lane path switch-

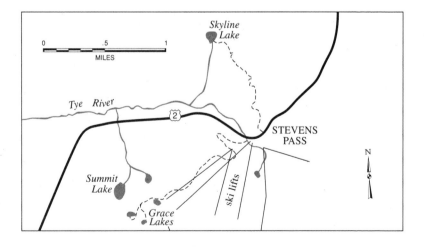

One of the Grace Lakes

backs steeply across open huckleberry slopes (rich with berries in the fall if you get there in time) with increasing views out over the highway and ski complex.

After the rut passes a lookoutlike tower, bear left on what suddenly becomes a real trail through heather and huckleberries, ending shortly at a small but pretty alpine lake worth, as promised, every groan and every step. Way paths lead here and there through alpine forest around the shore. Pick your own.

To reach Grace Lakes (more than 2 miles and up 1,100 feet), walk uphill into the ski area from the parking lot, taking the first ski area maintenance road uphill to the right beyond the maintenance shed. Follow the road beneath and beside the Green chairlift as it grinds its uninteresting way to the very top of the lift. Find the trail, finally, beyond and behind the lift.

A heather path drops immediately to the first small lake and then climbs over a small ridge to instant views of the third lake, dead ahead. But take a well-used spur trail across open heather slopes to the left to visit the pretty second lake before you return and proceed down to the third.

(The larger Summit Lake lies over a ridge to the right off the upper end of the third lake. The trail, however, is often lost in rockfalls.)

And please, don't rush from one lake to the next. Like diamonds, each of these lakes deserves your admiration and time to measure the individual beauties of each.

Lanham Lake and shoulder of Jim Hill Mountain

25 Lanham Lake

Features: forest and lake
One way: 1½ miles
Elevation gain: 1,100 feet
Difficulty: moderate to steep
Open: summer
Map: Green Trails 144

A short trail just off Highway 2 leads to a pleasant lake at 3,900 feet.

Drive east on Stevens Pass Highway 2 over Stevens Pass, turning right in about 6 miles to a snowpark area off Road 6960.

(Note: To return west toward the coast on Highway 2, turn right off Road 6960 into the eastbound lane of Highway 2 and then shortly left, downhill to the westbound lane.)

Find the signed trailhead east of Road 6960 in about 50 yards above the snowpark lot.

The path starts out in forest and in ½ mile breaks out into an ugly powerline right-of-way. Watch for trail signs or cairns or old tree blazes to pick your way beneath the lines to a trail again.

The path follows an old logging spur before entering a pleasant forest and climbing steadily near Lanham Creek to a pleasant picnic or camp spot on the lake. Can be busy on weekends.

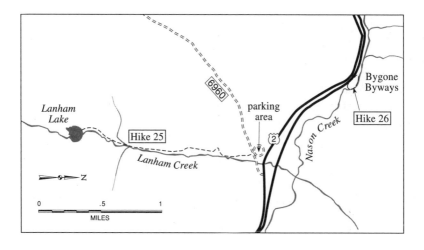

26   Bygone Byways

Features: history above a raging creek
One way: ¼-mile loop
Elevation gain: about 50 feet
Difficulty: easy
Open: spring to winter
Map: none

Walk above noisy Nason Creek to a glimpse of the early history of rail and road transportation across Stevens Pass. Part of historic roadside displays planned in the Stevens Pass Historic District.

(See Hike 21, Iron Goat Trail, and Hike 22, Deception Falls. Another display is planned on the old Stevens Pass Highway at the Wellington townsite, destroyed along with a passenger train in an avalanche in which 96 people were killed.)

Drive east on Stevens Pass Highway 2 over Stevens Pass, dropping to the left from the eastbound lane to the westbound lane of Highway 2 in about 6 miles (just beyond the snowpark area and Road 6960). Find the roadside display to the right (going west) in more than a mile. (See map on page 65.)

The path drops to a display board off the highway (get a brochure here) and then turns right down an old railroad bed blasted out of rock in 1892 by men who hand-drilled powder holes and then moved the blasted rock with horse-drawn scoops.

The section of railroad here was abandoned in 1929 after the present 8-mile tunnel was built through the pass. The rail right-of-way was incorporated for a time later as part of the first Cascade Scenic Highway.

The present-day path passes the collapsed remains of an old rock and earth oven used by railroad builders for baking bread and then along a section of a tote road over the pass, built to support construction of the railway.

Bygone Byways trail

27 Hidden Lake

Features: lake, forest, vistas
One way: about ½ mile
Elevation gain: 300 feet
Difficulty: short but steep
Open: spring to winter
Map: Green Trails 145

A short walk uphill past views over Lake Wenatchee leads to a pretty boulder-bound mountain lake.

Drive about 20 miles east of Stevens Pass on Stevens Pass Highway 2, turning left at Coles Corner onto Highway 207. In about 4 miles turn left toward Wenatchee State Park and Nason Creek Campground. At the entrance to Lake Wenatchee State Park, turn sharply left onto South Shore Road, driving to the end of Road 6607 at Glacier View Campground in less than 6 miles.

Find the trail uphill to the left at the end of the campground road leading directly to the lake. The well-worn path crosses a creek and then starts a steady and persistent climb through forest with glimpses now and then down on the lake and across at Dirty Face Mountain. Huckleberries along the way in the fall, if you get there before other hikers do.

The trail ends at a point that juts out into the water, offering

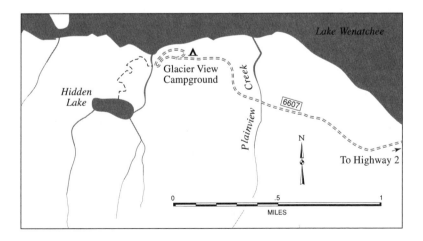

Hidden Lake

a full view of the lake. Unmaintained way trails lead both right and left along and above the shore. Explore them all, taking care to remember where it was you started so you can find the main trail back.

Tumbled rocks, some layered like huge birthday cakes, offer endless resting spots. Wonder as you rest where those rocks all tumbled from.

So bring a lunch, a magazine, a book, or a tape of music that only you can hear and enjoy. Early mornings and late summer evenings offer the best chance for solitude.

28 White River Falls

Features: waterfall, eroded rocks, forest
One way: less than 1 mile
Elevation gain: slight
Difficulty: easy
Open: summer
Map: Green Trails 145

If you want to meet this waterfall full face—and it's a face worth looking at—take a short walk down a wilderness trail.

Drive about 20 miles east of Stevens Pass on Stevens Pass Highway 2, turning left at Coles Corner onto Highway 207 and following it past Lake Wenatchee State Park and down the north shore of the lake. Bear right on White River Road 6400 at its junction with the Wenatchee River Road 6500. Drive 9 miles to the boundary of the Glacier Peak Wilderness Area.

Find the trail off the end of a large parking lot. The path immediately crosses a bridge above a White River rapids and enters the wilderness. In 100 feet take a path downriver to the left on a trail signed "Panther Creek and Mount David."

An old, blazed trail makes its way above the river through big cedars and Douglas fir to an unmarked but clear junction just short of a mile. The path to the left promptly snuggles up to

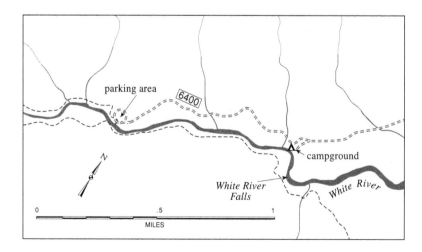

White River Falls

the edge of a ledge above the river and the waterfall. Two leaping torrents drop into a pool worked only by fisherman across the river. No crossing here either above or below the falls.

As signs warn, watch small children: There are no barriers. After you've admired the falls, also admire the wondrous patterns of erosion (note how even the highest boulder above the falls has been worn round by this torrent). Explore a spur path off the trail just upstream of the falls. More examples of erosion here and a view of a campground and campers across the stream. Again, do *not* attempt to cross the river no matter how docile the water seems.

The main wilderness trail continues downriver before climbing up Panther Creek. Another steep trail goes up Mount David.

Be sure to drive into the White River Campground as you leave. Walk over the outcrops you could see from across the river. Way trails lead downstream to the fishing holes and limited views of the falls.

29 Big Tree Loop

Features: ancient forest
One way: ½-mile loop, maybe more
Elevation gain: 100 feet
Difficulty: easy
Open: summer
Map: Green Trails 145

Walk around a shady loop through old-growth forest here where you can see whatever you take the time to see. No signs. No pamphlets. Just Mother Nature dressed in her best.

Drive about 20 miles east of Stevens Pass on Stevens Pass Highway 2, turning left at Coles Corner onto Highway 207 and following it past Lake Wenatchee State Park down the north shore of the lake. Beyond the forest ranger station, bear left on Wenatchee River Road 6500 at a junction with White River Road 6400. In about 7 miles from the junction, turn downhill to Soda Springs Campground. Find the trail off the uphill loop at the far end of the campground road.

The path drops down to a small bridge and into a grove of old cedars, Douglas fir, and hemlock decked out with devil's club, vine maples, ferns, and flowers in season.

Not a place to hurry through. If such forests are new to you,

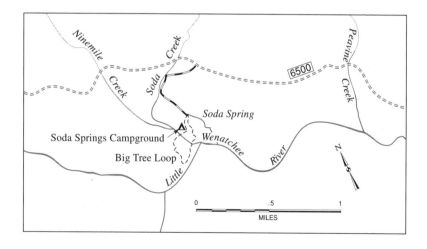

Little Wenatchee River from Big Tree Loop

take your plant book along so you can greet the plants you meet by name.

At the bottom of the loop, as the trail turns left, walk to the river straight ahead, return, and follow the main path through still-rich forest to another view of the river before the trail climbs gradually back to the campground.

Before you leave the campground, check the soda springs that gave the camp its name. Find the closest spring off the east side of the campground road across from the first camp site.

On an unmarked path beyond the spring, and to the right, note a large, soft sandstone boulder etched with initials that's been used as a campground "register" for years. Take time to "sign in" too.

Other springs can be found on unmarked paths above and along the river.

30   Tumwater Pipeline Trail

Features: river and history
One way: 1 mile
Elevation gain: none
Difficulty: easy
Open: all year
Map: none

Hike an historic pipeline trail that once carried water to generators that powered Great Northern trains through the 8-mile Cascade tunnel.

The pipeline and generating plant were abandoned after the railroad switched from pollution-free electricity to diesel fuel, which required the installation of giant fans in the tunnel to blow out the fumes.

Drive east on Stevens Pass Highway 2 into Tumwater Canyon, turning right toward the Wenatchee River on a short road leading to the river's edge halfway between Mileposts 97 and 98.

Find the trailhead off a parking lot, site of the one-time generating plant. Follow the path upriver, crossing a steel bridge that once held the water pipes. At ¾ mile stop at a delightful sandbar with views across the river to Castle Rock, where climbers often practice on the near-vertical rock faces there.

At 1 mile the path comes to an abrupt end at a cliff. Evi-

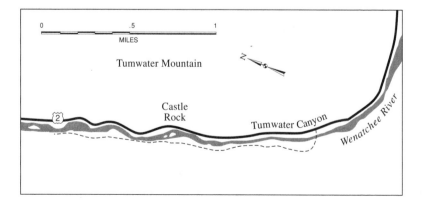

Wenatchee River and Castle Rock

dently the pipeline tunneled through rock here. A massive rockslide now blocks the opening.

Carry binoculars for watching climbers across the river and be alert for rattlesnakes.

Chatter Bridge over Icicle Creek

31 Icicle Gorge

Features: vistas, forest, rushing creek
One way: 1 mile or more
Elevation gain: very little
Difficulty: easy
Open: summer
Map: Green Trails 177

Start with a high view of a roaring stream and then drop into old forest to wander along what's now a busy, chattering creek.

Drive east on Stevens Pass Highway 2 to Leavenworth, turning south (right) onto Icicle Road as the highway approaches the edge of town. Follow the road into the Wenatchee National Forest (now Road 76) and then on to the Chatter Creek Guard Station.

Find the trailhead across the road from the guard station. The trail drops from a parking area on the creek side of the road to a bridge high above a narrow cleft filled with bowls and streamlined slabs carved by noisy Icicle Creek, which tumbles wildly through this gorge all year long.

Beyond the bridge the trail continues upriver across several rock ledges (to the right) that provide views up and down the busy creek.

Beyond the bluffs the trail drops to the water's edge through rich old forest and across small creeks (which may be flooded in the spring) to small sandy beaches with plenty of picnic and resting places.

Continue your explorations as far as the trail continues with fresh coves, eroded rocks, forest, and river vistas. The path was expected to be completed through to the Rock Island Bridge in 1993.

(Historic notes: This path, once known as Icicle Creek Bridle Trail, stretched unimpeded to the Rock Island Bridge until private logging closed the upper end. The trail to Windy Pass and Trout Lake once took off from this path, too. In fact, that was the reason for the bridge. This trail now starts from Rock Island and, due to more logging, naturally, climbs above the original trail, in fact, almost up to the wilderness border to avoid new clearcuts.)

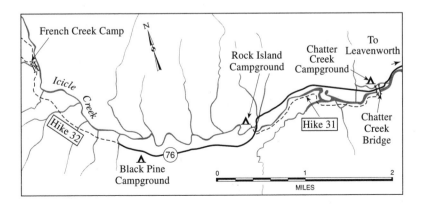

32 French Creek Camp

Features: forest and creek
One way: 1½ miles
Elevation gain: very slight
Difficulty: easy
Open: summer
Map: Green Trails 177

Take an easy walk through a shady forest up Icicle Creek to a noisy little rapids and pleasant camping spot.

Drive east on Stevens Pass Highway 2 to Leavenworth, turning south (right) onto Icicle Road as the highway approaches the edge of town. Follow the road into the Wenatchee National Forest (now Road 76) and past the Chatter Creek Guard Station. In less than 2 miles, follow the road left across the creek and then on to its end in another 2 miles. (See map on page 77.)

The trail starts off the end of a parking area and proceeds straight-away toward French Creek and a well-used camping spot.

But, again, do not rush, for there's nothing here to hurry for. Rather, enjoy the forest and listen—yes, listen—to the hustling creek off to your right. For before you reach the camp you'll hear a busy rapids there. Wander through the woods—you'll not get lost—and find a series of modest rapids worth seeing and, yes, listening to. Some contend you can sometimes hear voices of the past whispering to you as you wait. The spirits of hikers or explorers who came this way before? Judge from what they say to you.

The French Creek Camp is a good destination for a test-run backpack trip. It's busy on most weekends, however.

French Creek

33 Peshastin Pinnacles State Park

Features: rocky spires and mountaineers
One way: as far as you want to walk
Elevation gain: the choice is yours
Difficulty: easy to beyond belief
Open: closed in winter
Map: trail map posted at the park

The opportunities in this state park are endless, but the limitations are severe. You can walk on loops among this host of barren spires as far as you like with no problem at all. But to climb them? You'll need lessons, most certainly.

Drive east on Stevens Pass Highway 2 (or I-90 and Highway 97) beyond the towns of Peshastin and Dryden (4 miles west of Cashmere) to Peshastin Pinnacles State Park on the north side of the highway. Follow signs through orchards and across an irrigation ditch to the large parking lot just below the unlikely group of barren spires—the Peshastin Pinnacles.

The trail begins at a signed display and then climbs to trails that lead to a series of loops past the base of Dinosaur Tower (the farthest), Vulture Slab, Orchard Rock, Grand Central Tower, Martian Slab, and Austrian Slab, to name a few.

This park of nothing more than cracks and slabs has been

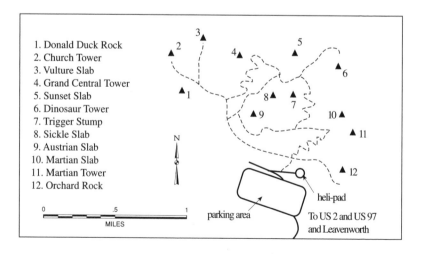

1. Donald Duck Rock
2. Church Tower
3. Vulture Slab
4. Grand Central Tower
5. Sunset Slab
6. Dinosaur Tower
7. Trigger Stump
8. Sickle Slab
9. Austrian Slab
10. Martian Slab
11. Martian Tower
12. Orchard Rock

N

0   .5   1
MILES

parking area

heli-pad

To US 2 and US 97
and Leavenworth

Climber on a Peshastin Pinnacle

used for years by rock climbers as a place to learn and test their skills belaying, rappelling, climbing slabs, jamming holds, and working cracks with their static and dynamic ropes and assorted tools like carabiners, cams, nuts, tubers, hammers, brakes, harnesses, and shoes.

Not that you have to climb here to enjoy this park. Just watching and listening can be exciting, too, as climbers talk each other across this face or up that crack in places that seem impossible to go.

So walk, see, and listen, remembering not to interfere with those climbing or with their ropes that sometimes dangle loosely on the trail, and stand clear of all the rocks in case some piece of climbing hardware happens to be dropped.

34 Clara and Marion Lakes

Features: mountain lakes in lava scree
One way: a long mile
Elevation gain: about 900 feet
Difficulty: steep
Open: summer
Map: Wenatchee National Forest map

A twin surprise: two small mountain lakes surrounded by ponderosa pine set in bowls of lava scree typical of the mountains here.

Drive east to Wenatchee on either Stevens Pass Highway 2 or I-90 and Highway 97, following signs straight through town to the Mission Ridge Ski Resort, 12 miles from the edge of town. Great views of the Columbia River valley and Wenatchee from the road.

Find the trail, marked as the "Squilchuck Trail/Lake Clara," uphill to the right where the paved road first enters the ski area parking lot.

Trail bikes are permitted on the first section of the trail, as ruts in the path and trenches on steep switchbacks attest.

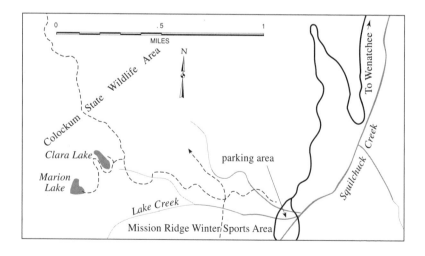

Clara Lake

At a T junction, signed with trail uses but not directions, turn left on a broad path that serves snowmobiles in the winter and then sharply uphill to the right in a few yards.

The path now climbs through pleasant forest (no motor bikers allowed now) to a second T junction. Turn left here, cross a creek, pass a shallow, narrow pond, and shortly reach the outlet of Clara Lake.

Pleasant places to camp and picnic in the trees or in the sun on both sides of the lake, at 5,500 feet.

To reach Marion Lake cross the outlet at Clara Lake, walk up the lake to a clump of trees, and take a ¼-mile trail that traverses back uphill over a ridge and down to Marion Lake, also at 5,500 feet, set in a bowl of its own.

Linger near either or both. Such pleasantness is hard to find.

Storm-bent tree

35 Saddle Lake

Features: lake and meadows
One way: 2-plus miles
Elevation gain: 700 feet
Difficulty: steep and rough
Open: summer
Maps: Green Trails 109, 110

Struggle 2 miles to a subalpine lake that marks the entrance to an inspiring world of alpine meadows.

From I-5 in Everett turn east at Exit 194 onto Highway 2 (from Highway 405 turn off at Exit 23 to Highway 522), turning north in both instances onto Highway 9. In about 6 miles north of Highway 2, turn east on Highway 92 to Granite Falls, another 8 miles, and the beginning of Mountain Loop Highway.

In about 7 miles from Granite Falls (4 miles *west* of the Verlot Information Center), turn north (left) onto Forest Road 41, following the road some 17 miles to Tupso Pass. Find the trail at the end of Spur Road 4160.

The trail enters the Boulder River Wilderness and promptly begins its rooted and eroded struggle up switchbacks to a ridge (vistas now and then) to Saddle Lake at 3,780 feet.

Admire the lake with its marsh-loving flowers and scurrying salamanders and then press on at least another mile (this path is not so rough) to the first of many rolling meadows tucked with tarns.

Find your own hummock of heather and give thanks to the hundreds who did political battle to preserve this corner of heaven.

For further thanks in an even bigger corner of this paradise, hike another 1½ miles to Goat Flats—a decorated altar of nature's splendors. And treat all these tarns and meadows with the respect due any place of worship. No open fires.

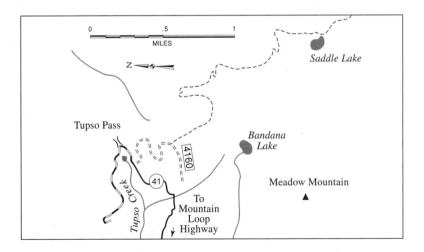

36 Mount Pilchuck Lookout

Features: vistas from 5,300 feet
One way: 3 miles
Elevation gain: 2,200 feet
Difficulty: very steep, but short, boulder field
Open: snow often until late summer
Map: Green Trails 109

Vistas here from the Olympics to the Cascades plus every-thing in between. But not for the timid or the unprepared.

To reach Mountain Loop Highway, drive north on Highway 9 for 6 miles from Highway 2 or south 12 miles from Arlington to Highway 92 and then east to Granite Falls in 8 more miles.

From Granite Falls follow Mountain Loop Highway a little more than 12 miles to the Verlot Information Center. Turn right (south) onto Road 42 in another mile (just beyond the bridge over the south fork of the Stillaguamish River), driving about 7 miles to a large parking area. Find the trail uphill to the right at the beginning of the parking lot.

The path climbs most of the way in forest with glimpses of surrounding country through the trees and then loses elevation as it works its way around cliffs.

Don't be lured by well-worn jogs in the trail that may seem

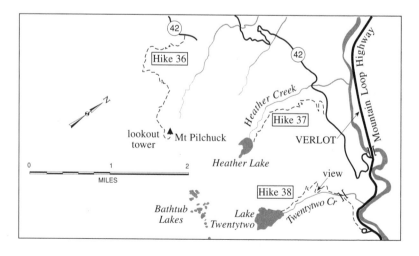

Mount Pilchuck Lookout

like time-saving shortcuts through boulder fields. No way. First, the rock fields can be dangerous. And second, you may very well lose your way, particularly coming down with few cairns to guide you. These unmarked slopes are pocked with cliffs.

The trail ends in a final series of switchbacks that climb 100 feet to a final pile of giant boulders topped with the lookout. Pick your way to the building with care.

Again, stick with the trail, avoid the lure of shortcuts across the boulder fields, and use the time you saved to enjoy what you see. Take a highway map to identify what you're looking at (a forest map will help but is much too small).

The trail starts in the national forest and ends in state park land.

Heather Lake

37 Heather Lake

Features: pretty mountain lake
One way: 2 miles
Elevation gain: 1,000 feet
Difficulty: moderate to steep
Open: summer
Map: Green Trails 109

Hike through old forest, past a small waterfall, to an alpine lake tucked in a cirque on the side of Pilchuck Mountain.

On Highway 9 drive north 6 miles from Highway 2 or south 12 miles from Arlington to Highway 92 and then east to Granite Falls in 8 more miles.

From Granite Falls follow Mountain Loop Highway a little more than 12 miles to the Verlot Information Center. Turn right (south) in another mile onto Road 42 (just beyond the bridge over the south fork of the Stillaguamish River). Find the trail to the left in less than 1.5 miles, uphill across from a parking area on the right side of the road. (See map on page 86.)

The path (no longer up an old logging road) starts out with a series of short switchbacks up a stream draw through maturing second-growth forest. Note the huge old stumps of trees, 6 to 10 feet in diameter, logged here early in the century by men who stood on springboards jammed into the notches you can still see in the stumps.

The trail joins a stretch of the old road but shortly resumes its traillike ways, climbing to a small waterfall (catch your breath here) and then switchbacking again before dropping to the lake at 2,450 feet.

Limited camping is permitted here away from the lakeshore. Informal trails lead to other points around the lake. A lot of rocks to sit on for watching and listening to what Nature has secreted here.

38   Lake Twentytwo

Features: waterfalls and lake
One way: 2½ miles or less
Elevation gain: 1,200 feet or less
Difficulty: steep
Open: summer
Maps: Green Trails 109, 110

A hike to the lake is certainly worth the effort, but a walk halfway through a lovely forest past waterfalls is a worthy effort, too.

On Highway 9 drive north 6 miles from Highway 2 or south 12 miles from Arlington to Highway 92 and then east to Granite Falls in 8 more miles.

From Granite Falls follow Mountain Loop Highway a little more than 12 miles to the Verlot Information Center. Find the trailhead in less than 2 miles at the end of a short spur road loop to the right. (See map on page 86.)

The path almost immediately enters a research natural area that, except for the damage created by humans along the trail, has evolved untouched as a lush old-growth forest filled with fallen moss-covered giants, old trees straddling rocks, and seedlings bursting from rotting logs, amid an abundance of salmonberries, maidenhair, deer and lady ferns, devil's club, bunchberry, skunk cabbages, and even shy single delights on mossy logs—only to begin a list.

Note, too, as you walk this beginning section of trail how even in the driest years little streams bubble from rocks above the path, demonstrating how the established and undisturbed forest stabilizes water runoff which dries up early in the summer on logged-off trails.

The trail winds above the highway for an easy ½ mile to a bridge over Twentytwo Creek. Pause here for sure to enjoy the beauty of the busy little waterfalls and to follow short way paths through the pools and giant cedar trees.

Beyond the creek the trail starts its stiff and persistent upward climb toward the lake in another 2 miles. Half that distance, however, will reward you with still more opportunities to admire trees, shrubs, and flowers before coming face to face with a pretty full-scale, two-step waterfall. For many, that may be destination enough.

For those who climb on, though, a pretty lake lies at 2,460 feet with an almost permanent snowfield at the end. On weekends, of course, hundreds of people, too. No open fires are permitted here. And, please, treat the fragile lakeshore most tenderly.

Lake Twentytwo

Pinnacle Lake

39 Bear and Pinnacle Lakes

Features: lakes and forest
One way: 2 miles or less
Elevation gain: up to 1,200 feet
Difficulty: moderate to steep
Open: midsummer
Maps: Green Trails 109, 110

An easy ¼-mile walk leads to one mountain lake set in forest. An added 2-mile uphill struggle leads to another set in a heather cirque. And both are worth the trip.

On Highway 9 drive north 6 miles from Highway 2 or south 12 miles from Arlington to Highway 92 and then east to Granite Falls in 8 more miles.

From Granite Falls, drive east on Mountain Loop Highway

92 past the Verlot Information Station and Gold Bar Campground. About 2.5 miles beyond the campground, turn (right) south on Road 4020, turning right in another 1.7 miles onto Road 4021 and following it to the trailhead in about 4 more miles.

The trail starts with a short, steep pitch that ends in about 50 feet at the base of a huge cedar snag and then continues on to a junction. Turn right at the trail junction in a few hundred yards to reach Bear Lake (2,775 feet) and left to Pinnacle Lake in another 2 miles.

The trail to Bear Lake follows a ridge with views over the logged off Stillaguamish Valley before dropping through open forest past several camp spots on two levels above the lake.

No sandy beaches here, but a muddy wade will lead to a midday swim in warm water over icy springs. Watch for ospreys fishing here. Fishermen paths lead around the lake.

The trail to Pinnacle Lake, which can be soggy in the spring, climbs to views over Bear Lake, topping out across a series of marshy flower and huckleberry meadows before reaching the lake (3,800 feet) surrounded by patches of timber, more meadows, and scenic rock bluffs. Treat the meadows here with kindness so others after you may enjoy them too.

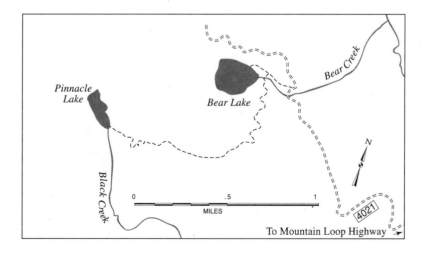

40   Lake Evan and Boardman Lake

Features: rich forest and lovely lakes
One way: 1 mile
Elevation gain: 200 feet
Difficulty: easy to moderate
Open: summer
Map: Green Trails 110

Two mountain lakes in less than a mile, plus grand old-growth forest worth the trip all by itself.

On Highway 9 drive north 6 miles from Highway 2 or south 12 miles from Arlington to Highway 92 and then east to Granite Falls in 8 more miles.

From Granite Falls, drive east on Mountain Loop Highway 92 past the Verlot Information Station and Gold Bar Campground. In about 2.5 miles beyond the campground, turn south on Road 4020, reaching the trailhead (views over the valley en route) in about 4.7 miles. Find a parking area as the road jogs sharply to the west.

Find the heavily used trail beyond the downroad side of Evan Creek. The path reaches Lake Evan (2,751 feet) with its soggy but heavily used camping spots in less than 50 yards beyond a grove of old cedar trees.

To reach Boardman Lake (2,981 feet) take the trail uphill

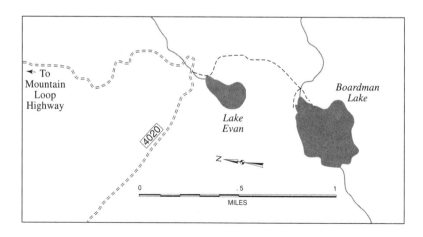

Boardman Lake

through a lush, open forest of old-growth Douglas fir, hemlock, and cedars that have grown here for hundreds of years. Wonder as you stand in awe below them: Could the two or three seedlings that loggers promise to plant should they be cut truly ever replace them? In the 50 years they brag about? Never. In 200 years—at the end of six generations, for your great-great-great-great grandchildren? At this elevation? Probably not even then.

The trail crests a ridge above the outlet creek and then drops to the lake. Go either right or left for picnic or camping spots. The trail to the left crosses the outlet and then circles a rocky knoll.

No warning seems necessary here. The trail is wide and easy to follow. Yet each year novice hikers lose their way trying the return to the road. So: Note where the trail reaches the lake and if you decide to return to the car alone have a friend verify your starting path on the well-worn trail.

41 Kelcema Lake

Features: mountain lake
One way: less than ½ mile
Elevation gain: slight
Difficulty: easy
Open: midsummer
Map: Green Trails 110

A narrow and steep road leads to an easy trail to a popular lake just inside the Boulder River Wilderness.

On Highway 9 drive north 6 miles from Highway 2 or south 12 miles from Arlington to Highway 92 and then east to Granite Falls in 8 more miles.

From Granite Falls drive east on Mountain Loop Highway 92 turning north on Road 4052 about 1 mile beyond (east of) Silverton. (The road is sometimes not signed at the highway nor along the road itself.) Find the trail in about 4.5 miles up a view road that can be rough beyond a "paved" crossing of Deer Creek.

The trail begins on the left side of the road at a point where the road turns sharply right. The path winds through a soggy meadow and open forest to the lake at 3,182 feet in a cirque at the base of Bald Mountain to the south.

Long before the road was built, this area was used as a Boy Scout camp. Nature now slowly heals itself. But don't let past human abuses now excuse your own. Campsites in well-worn places among the rocks.

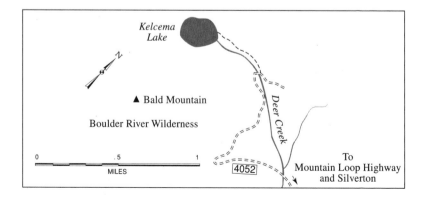

Kelcema Lake

Big Four Ice Cave

42 Big Four Ice Caves

Features: ice caves
One way: 1 mile
Elevation gain: 200 feet
Difficulty: moderate
Open: summer
Map: Green Trails 110

Ice caves! What else is there to say? Caves (some years just one) etched by streams beneath the snow and ice of a not-quite glacier at the shaded base of Big Four Mountain that commands this section of Mountain Loop Highway.

From Granite Falls, 8 miles east of Highway 9, drive east on Mountain Loop Highway 15 miles beyond the Verlot Information

Center to a display and trailhead at the end of a short, marked spur road to the right.

Find a great spectacle here even if you don't walk the mile trail to the ice caves. A hotel once occupied this site, built in 1922 for tourists brought in by train. It burned in 1949. A chimney is all that now remains.

As you stand in the developed hotel clearing now you can still see why they built the resort here and wonder, truly, why it failed. Now as then, waterfalls plume in strings from Big Four's cliffs. Now as then, birds sing in the underbrush and trees. Now as then, beaver try to dam the river, and now as then, they are just as difficult to see.

The trail to the ice caves, however, is probably much better now. A planked walkway now leads across the soggy meadow at the trail's start, and a sturdy bridge now crosses the creek to the caves at the trail's end.

With the same warning now, most certainly, as hotel guests got then: The caves, not usually open until mid-July or later, are hazardous, as is the snowfield above them. The snow and ice here fall from mountain cliffs in the winter. Rocks fall from the cliffs in the summer. So explore with caution. Check with the Verlot Information Station about current conditions and obey any and all warning signs.

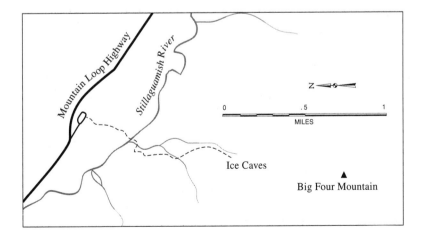

43 Independence and Coal Lakes

Features: lakes and old forest
One way: ¾ mile but seems much farther
Elevation gain: 200 feet (counting the ups and downs)
Difficulty: steep and rough
Open: summer
Map: Green Trails 110

Independence Lake is the goal here—with Coal Lake an extra prize. Plus—yes, plus—spectacular airplane views of Big Four Mountain and the Stillaguamish Valley from the ever-climbing road.

From Granite Falls, 8 miles east of Highway 9, drive east on Mountain Loop Highway about 15.5 miles beyond the Verlot Information Center, turning left (north) to Road 4060 (the first road beyond the road to the well-signed Ice Caves). The junction may not be signed, and there may be no forest road numbers posted on the road. Stop at a formal viewpoint in about 3 miles. (See the sights and then look for black leaf-imprinted rocks in ancient shale across the road.)

The road passes a Coal Lake parking strip on the left at about 4.5 miles, reaching the end of the road and the Independence Lake trailhead parking area in another twisty, uphill 0.25 mile.

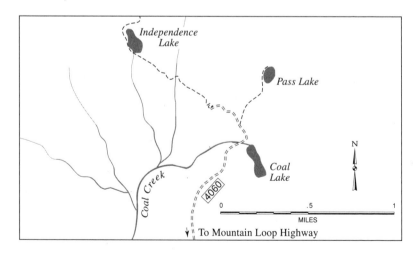

Independence Lake

Find the trail to Independence Lake uphill from the road-end parking lot. Again, there may be no signs. The path starts out in an old clearcut but shortly enters a cool and shady old-growth forest.

Once it enters the old forest, the trail reverts to history. Probably built by the depression-years Civilian Conservation Corps in the 1930s, the path is largely unchanged. Following still-visible, overgrown blazes on trees, the trail drops down to a creek, makes its way back up again, goes level for a while to another creek, and then climbs sharply in lunging spurts over roots and rocks to the jewel of a lake at 3,700 feet.

Resting slabs beside the outlet creek make the whole trip worthwhile. Listen here for the grouse, chatter of the squirrels and chipmunks, and one-note trill of the varied thrush.

The trail continues on around the crystal blue lake to an open meadow with camp spots in the trees.

And, yes, as you drive back take time to walk the few short yards from the road over a ledge to the narrow, snow-fed Coal Lake, surrounded by steep rock and timber slopes, at 3,420 feet. If you brought your kayak, canoe, or rubber raft: Enjoy!

44 Barlow Point

Features: vistas
One way: 1¼ miles
Elevation gain: 800 feet
Difficulty: moderate to very steep
Open: summer
Map: Green Trails 111

Walk an easy quarter mile and then climb a steep switchback mile to views out over the Stillaguamish Valley, down on Monte Cristo Lakes, and out at Big Four, Dickerman, and Sheep mountains.

From Granite Falls drive east on Mountain Loop Highway about 19.4 miles beyond the Verlot Information Center to Barlow Pass. Park either on the highway or in a small parking area at the end of a short spur road to the left. Find the trail off the parking area.

The path starts out on a gradual traverse through forest before turning right to begin the grinding switchback climb to the rocky site of an abandoned lookout at 3,200 feet.

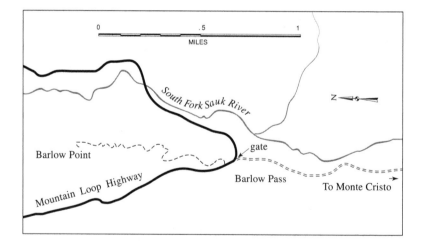

Barlow Point trailhead

The first section of the walk follows part of the bed of the railroad that once led to the long-defunct, but still private, Monte Cristo mining complex at the end of the now-gated county road (to the right) at the pass. The trail once continued down the railroad grade above the highway toward Silverton for almost 2 miles.

No water, naturally.

North Fork Falls

45 North Fork Sauk

Features: a waterfall and old-growth forest
One way: 2 miles or less
Elevation gain: 200 feet
Difficulty: Moderate
Open: early spring
Map: Green Trails 111

The best is the closest and easiest here. First, the North Fork waterfall as you start your drive up the north fork of the Sauk River. And then the wander through the lush forest near the primitive Sloan Creek Campground.

From Seattle drive north on I-5, turn east at Exit 208, and follow Highway 530 through Arlington to Darrington. Turn south in Darrington to Mountain Loop Forest Road 20, driving about 18 miles (or about 7 miles north of Barlow Pass if you start the loop from Granite Falls) to North Fork Road 49, sharply uphill to the east, just north of the North Fork Guard Station.

In a mile, park and hike down a steep but short trail (less than ¼ mile) to see North Fork falls. Find the trail off a small parking area on the right side of the road. A torrent all year and a tumult in the spring. Take your camera. The trail ends at a viewpoint. Stay on the trail.

Drive another 6 miles from the falls to a spur road to the left into the primitive Sloan Creek Campground. (If you cross the bridge over the river you've gone too far.)

Step out of your car and immerse yourself in a lush pocket of grand and ancient old-growth Douglas fir and cedar trees and old snags pecked full of holes, all rising out of a lush understory of ferns, devil's club, twisted stalk, and foam flowers—just to start a list.

Walk 100 yards or so down the North Fork trail to find a rusty salt-lick mineral seep off to the left in a skunk cabbage garden where animals come to drink the witches' brew. Animal tracks—and deer if you're lucky—all of the time.

The trail continues up the North Fork entering the Glacier Peak Wilderness in about ½ mile. Once in the wilderness the path climbs away from the river across old avalanche tracks with views occasionally up to Sloan Peak. Walk as far as you want.

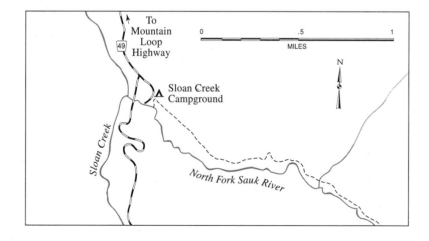

46   Beaver Lake

Features: beaver ponds
One way: 3 miles but you need not go that far
Elevation gain: very little
Difficulty: easy
Open: all year
Map: Green Trails 111

An easy 2-mile walk over an old abandoned logging railroad grade leads to a small beaver lake and a haven for birds and other wildlife.

From Seattle drive north on I-5, turn east at Exit 208, and follow Highway 530 through Arlington to Darrington. Turn south in Darrington to Mountain Loop Forest Road 20.

At 10 miles cross the Sauk River and find the trail off a short spur road to the right just beyond the river bridge and across from the junction with Forest Road 23 and its bridge over the White Chuck River to the abandoned White Chuck Campground.

Beaver here. Wood ducks, goldeneyes, deer, and mallards—if you are quiet and careful.

The path starts south out of the parking area on an old railroad grade built in 1914 (you'll find signs of an old trestle later

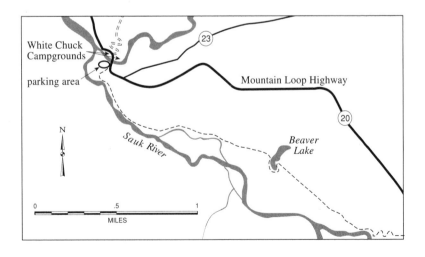

Old railroad trestle at Beaver Lake

on), passing through an alder forest logged early in the century but that never restored itself. Occasional big hemlocks and cedar trees with a virtual feast of salmonberries amongst the nettles in early summer.

Shortly, the trail drops to the left of the railroad grade to follow a sometimes soggy off-and-on puncheon path to a small bridge and pond and your first glimpses of the beavers' work. Old overgrown dams for sure and small signs of current beaver upkeep and repair on weakening sections of the pond. With lush groves of old cedars to the right.

Wander old beaver dam–top paths until they reach the open river and start uphill to the left. Turn back.

47 Old Sauk River Trail

Features: grand old-growth forest plus a river
One way: 3 miles complete
Elevation gain: none
Difficulty: easy
Open: all year
Map: Green Trails 110

A 3-mile walk will take you from one entrance to the other. But a wander as far as you want to go from either end is worth every step you take.

And note: It is the ancient forest here, not the river, that commands attention, even when shouting kayakers drift past from their upriver landing near the old White Chuck Campground.

From Seattle drive north on I-5, turn east at Exit 208, and follow Highway 530 through Arlington to Darrington. Turn south in Darrington to Mountain Loop Forest Road 20.

Find the northern entrance to the trail south of Darrington to the left of the loop highway about 0.7 mile beyond the bridge over Clear Creek and Clear Creek Campground. Watch for a hiker trail sign.

Find the southern entrance hiker trail sign in another 3 miles, or, coming on the loop highway from the south, about 2.5 miles from the bridge over the Sauk River. Also marked with a hiker trail sign.

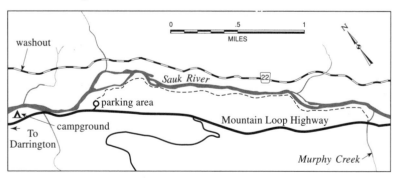

Sauk River

At the northern end the trail starts from a parking area in the trees east of the highway. At the southern end the path drops from the road along the north side of Murphy Creek.

The entire trail here winds across a large, old floodplain just a few feet above the Sauk River through continuing groves of old-growth cedar and hemlock filled with arches of moss-draped vine maple. Forest flowers here in season: in the spring, star flowers, trilliums, and lilies, with bunchberries, red-tasseled devil's club, and blossoming pipsissewas in the fall. With sword ferns, deer ferns, and licorice ferns, of course.

The Sauk River, which created this floodplain hundreds of years ago, as the age of the trees here testifies, now cuts the bank away as it swings back and forth across its wide riverbed, eroding ever-changing channels and exposing monster boulders that will cause you to ask from whence they came.

48 Boulder Falls

Features: waterfalls and old-growth forest
One way: 1¼ miles
Elevation gain: 200 feet
Difficulty: easy with one short grade
Open: early spring to late fall
Maps: Green Trails 77, 109

Walk through lush forest to double wisps of water pluming off a cliff into the raging Boulder River in the Boulder River Wilderness.

From Seattle drive north on I-5, turn east at Exit 208, and follow Highway 530 through Arlington to Milepost 41, about 8 miles west of Darrington.

At the milepost sign turn south onto what is sometimes signed as French Creek Road 2010, driving past an abandoned campground to the end of the road in 4 miles.

Find the trail off the end of the parking area. Trail sign in about 100 yards.

The path starts on an overgrown logging road through verdant alder forest with only glimpses of the river through the trees. The trail remains level until it turns uphill, climbing past a camp spot and skeleton of an old shelter well above the river to the right.

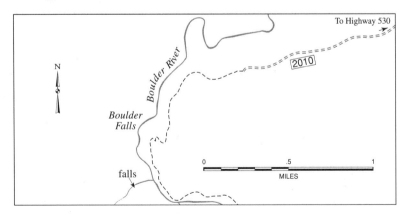

Boulder River and unnamed falls

At the wilderness boundary the path enters old-growth forest, but stays well above the river. Listen for the real Boulder Falls out of sight below you in the gully. (No trail.)

You'll hear the popular unnamed double falls (often thought of as Boulder Falls) plunging from its cliff well before you reach a resting log with a full view of the falls directly across the river. Walk to an open area in another 50 yards to find way paths down to the river and new perspectives of the falls, which flow all summer even in the driest years. Another path drops to the river just before you reach the resting log but offers no views of the falls.

49 Twin Lakes

Features: lakes and forest
One way: 2¼ miles
Elevation gain: 200 feet
Difficulty: moderate
Open: all year
Map: Moran State Park brochure

A gentle trail winds along the shore of one lake before climbing gradually up a cool, shallow valley to two pleasant, smaller mountain lakes.

Take the state ferry at the end of North Cascades Highway 20 in Anacortes. From the Orcas Island ferry landing, follow signs for 13 miles on Olga Road through East Sound to Moran State Park. From the park entrance continue along the shore of Cascade Lake toward Olga, turning uphill to the left in 1.5 miles onto the road to Mount Constitution (be sure to visit the vista tower there) and then right on a spur road to Mountain Lake in another mile. Find the trail to the left of the boat ramp in Mountain Lake Campground.

The path ambles along the west shore of the lake around coves and points mostly near the water, through groves of old trees and past unmarked paths to viewpoints and picnic spots.

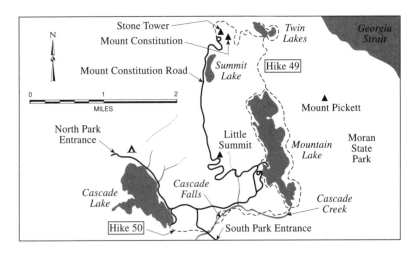

Mountain Lake

At one point the trail skirts a blowdown area, which illustrates the violence of the winter storms that sometimes sweep the island. At another point it passes a meadow, site of someone's home in the past.

At the upper end of the lake, in a little more than 1¼ miles, the trail drops down to a bridge and trail junction: left to Twin Lakes, right around Mountain Lake.

The broad Twin Lakes path now makes its way gradually upward through rich forest, past a rocky cliff, always within earshot of a busy creek, to another junction in about ¾ mile in a grand stand of ancient Douglas fir and young hemlock surrounded by ferns and flowers with pileated woodpeckers and grazing deer.

Turn right to both lakes and the small stream that connects them. (The trail continuing ahead climbs sharply about 1¼ miles through second-growth forest with few views to the stone tower atop Mount Constitution.)

Stop between the Twin Lakes and enjoy the forest and view of the lakes, or take trails across a wooden bridge: left around the little lake in about ½ mile or right around the larger in more than ½ mile.

50 Mountain Lake to Cascade Lake

Features: waterfalls and forest
One way: about 3 plus miles
Elevation loss: 570 feet
Difficulty: moderate
Open: all year
Map: Moran State Park brochure

Waterfalls and rich old forest: all along a single trail that drops from Mountain Lake to Cascade Lake. Have someone drop you off at the top and pick you up at the bottom.

Take the state ferry at the end of North Cascades Highway 20 in Anacortes. From the Orcas Island ferry landing, follow signs for 13 miles on Olga Road through East Sound to Moran State Park. From the park entrance continue along the shore of Cascade Lake toward Olga, turning uphill to the left in 1.5 miles onto the road to Mount Constitution and then right on a spur road to Mountain Lake in another mile. (See map on page 112.)

Find the signed trail off the right-hand side of the road as you first reach the Mountain Lake landing complex.

The path winds through forest, dropping below the lake's outlet dam in less than a mile. At the dam the trail drops downhill on the left side of the outlet stream (deer here in all of the unexpected places), crossing back to the right in another quarter mile. At the end of 1½ miles, the path crosses a bridge at the end of a meadow surrounded by old alder and breaks out on a road. In another long ¼ mile turn left downhill off the road onto a trail signed to Cavern, Rustic, and Cascade falls.

The trail now switchbacks down to above the first falls (way trails lead to closer looks) and passes through a grove of impressive cedars and Douglas firs soaking their roots near the creek before reaching the second falls at the end of 1¾ miles.

At Cascade Falls, the largest, in another few hundred yards, the trail drops past a series of three cascades, all with informal viewing points.

A warning here: Well-used view places on rocks near the falls should be picked with care. Moss-covered rocks can be dangerous and slippery when wet. Not a place for children.

To continue to Cascade Lake, take the lower, well-developed trail along the wooden rail (uphill paths lead to a parking area on the road). The trail drops through still more groves of ancient trees before reaching the highway.

At the highway turn right and in about 100 yards (look back over your shoulder here to see an osprey nest atop a stub tree) cross to a parking area and a gated road that leads back to the Cascade Lake ranger station and campground.

Cascade Falls

51 Mount Young

Features: vistas and historic site
One way: 1 mile
Elevation gain: about 600 feet
Difficulty: short but steep
Open: all year
Map: San Juan Island National Historical Park brochure

Views over farms, bays, and inlets at Haro Strait and out over the Olympics from atop a glacier-rounded "mountain." With a quiet reminder of the violence of the beautiful surrounding sea in a small military cemetery en route.

Take the state ferry at the end of North Cascades Highway 20 in Anacortes. From the San Juan Island ferry terminal in Friday Harbor, follow signs toward Roche Harbor. Turn south toward British Camp, the northern half of the San Juan Island National Historical Park, at a T junction in about 9 miles.

After visiting the garden and restored buildings of the British fort (the British here stood off a 66-man American army during a 12-year dispute over who had jurisdiction over the shooting of a pig), find the mountain trail through the trees off the end of the parking lot.

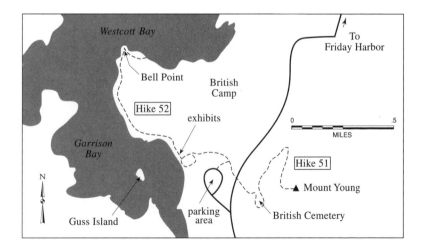

Garrison Bay and Haro Strait from Mount Young

The path climbs first to the highway, then on to a display board in ¼ mile, to the cemetery in less than ½ mile, and to the top of Mount Young at 650 feet at the end of a mile.

A gravel path ends at the small, shady cemetery, where one civilian and seven members of the Royal Marine Light Infantry lie buried, most victims not of war but of accidental drownings in the surrounding sea.

The trail beyond the cemetery climbs sharply through madrona and maple trees with occasional glimpses of the Strait, ending in a series of unmarked spurs to rock outcrop views. A display identifies features in the area at a formal overlook just below the summit.

The best views, naturally, are to be found on the rounded top of the mountain. Wander or rest here where you will, framing pictures both west of the Strait and south to the Olympics from the rocky knolls carved by glaciers.

Note where you entered the open area atop the mountain so you can return the way you came.

52 Bell Point

Features: seashore
One way: ½ mile
Elevation gain: none
Difficulty: easy
Open: all year
Map: San Juan Island National Historical Park brochure

An easy and pleasant forested trail winds along the shore of Garrison and Westcott bays off Haro Strait to a pleasant picnic and rest stop at Bell Point.

Take the state ferry at the end of North Cascades Highway 20 in Anacortes. From the San Juan Island ferry terminal in Friday Harbor, follow signs toward Roche Harbor, turning south toward British Camp, the northern half of the San Juan Island National Historical Park, at a T junction in about 9 miles. (See map on page 116.)

First, visit the garden and restored buildings of this nineteenth-century fort where the British faced a 66-man American army during a 12-year dispute over the arrest of an American settler who shot a British pig. A German kaiser finally settled the dispute by drawing the present Canadian–U.S. border through Haro Strait.

(But don't think that American and British settlers were the first to live on this bay. Archeologists, digging in middens along the shore, have found evidence that Native Americans lived on the island 1,500 years ago.)

To find the trail to Bell Point, walk across the parade ground in front of the restored blockhouse, hospital, commissary, and farmhouse toward Garrison Bay, finding the trailhead to the right (north).

The path winds near the shore through a forest of madrona and Douglas fir to the point that separates Garrison and Westcott bays and to views through the inlet into Haro Strait.

For information about digging shellfish on park shores, check with rangers for locations and limits.

English Camp from Bell Point trail

53 South Beach

Features: beach, birds, vistas
One way: about 1½ miles
Elevation gain: negligible
Difficulty: easy
Open: all year
Map: San Juan Island National Historical Park brochure

Beaches, yes. The longest public beach on San Juan Island. With birds, vistas, and tide pools galore.

Take the state ferry from the end of North Cascades Highway 20 in Anacortes. From the Friday Harbor ferry terminal, drive west on Spring Street, turning south on Mullis Road, continuing on Argyle Road, and turning right and then south on Cattle Point Road to American Camp, the southern section of San Juan Island National Historical Park, a total of 6 miles.

At the American Camp boundary, turn easterly on American Camp Road and, finally, south on Pickett's Lane to a beach spur road, picnic areas, and a parking area.

Your trail here is the beach and whichever way you want to walk: west over assorted headlands to Grandma's Cove or east on sand beach (or path above the beach) toward Cattle Point.

Constant vistas either way out over the Strait of Juan de Fuca of the Olympic Mountains, passing freighters, tugs with tows, cruising submarines, and, with luck, even Orca whales. With, at night, the glow of Victoria, British Columbia and Port

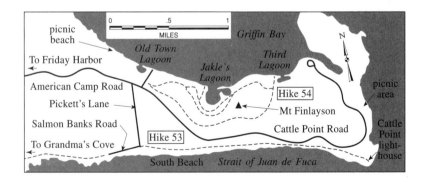

Cattle Point Lighthouse

Angeles and Port Townsend, and the flashing lighthouse signals from Ediz Hook, Dungeness Spit, Smith Island, and Port Wilson on Admiralty Inlet.

And the birds? Shorebirds of every sort: gulls, terns, plovers, turnstones, and greater and lesser yellowlegs. And over the shoreland: hawks and bald eagles, certainly. Even turkey vultures, with their bald, red heads, seldom seen elsewhere in western Washington.

With tide pools, too, at low tide near the headlands to the west. Choose what your spirit moves you to and spend whatever time you have.

Bald eagle near Jakle's Lagoon

 Jakle's Lagoon and Nature Trail

Features: forest, beach, vistas
One way: 1 mile plus
Elevation gain: 100 feet
Difficulty: moderate
Open: all year
Map: San Juan Island National Historical Park brochure

Two places here: the Jakle Farm, begun by an American soldier and his wife during the Pig War, now forest and wild meadowland, and Jakle's Cove on Griffin Bay, which was used by

Native Americans long before that "war." With the same marine life and birds now as then.

Take the state ferry from the end of North Cascades Highway 20 in Anacortes. From the Friday Harbor ferry terminal, drive west on Spring Street, turning south on Mullis Road, continuing on Argyle Road, and turning right and then south on Cattle Point Road to American Camp, the southern end of San Juan Island National Historical Park, a total of 6 miles.

At the American Camp boundary, turn easterly on American Camp Road to the trailhead parking lot just beyond the junction with Pickett's Lane. Find the trail to the right of the parking lot. (See map on page 120.)

The nature trail through the abandoned farm drops downhill past numbered posts through a forest of Douglas fir, hemlock, maple, alder, and an occasional now-much-talked-of yew, all undergrown with flowers, ferns, mosses, and berries.

The posts mark natural features on a loop developed by the San Juan Horticulture Society. If the display box is empty, obtain a guide booklet at Camp headquarters (on a spur road off Cattle Point Road at the point it turns east into American Camp Road).

In less than 1 mile the trail turns uphill to the right and enters the meadow with its different array of plants before turning back to the parking area.

To visit the beach with its views of both Mount Baker and Mount Rainier, take a spur trail left toward the water where the nature trail first levels out.

On the beach turn right to see Jakle's Lagoon in less than ½ mile. At the entrance to the lagoon, take time to examine the eroded bank. Note the thick layer of compressed seashell middens overgrown by sod. Here, Native Americans in the past ate the clams they harvested from the beach. Wonder, as you judge the thickness of the middens, how many years and how long ago they camped and feasted here.

Take time, too, to wander the beach and pools in the shallow lagoon, noting the tracks of animals and birds that graze and feast here even now. And listen also for the cries of eagles nesting in the forests near the beach. Watch them soar away as you approach.

Take the trail from the lagoon back to the forest/nature loop to return to the parking lot.

55 Rosario Head to Bowman Bay

Features: vistas and tide pools
One way: ½ mile
Elevation gain: about 100 feet
Difficulty: moderate to steep
Open: all year
Map: Deception Pass State Park brochure

Beaches, yes. Tide pools, too. But vistas on a sunny day that define everything Northwest beauty is all about.

Start from parking lots either at Bowman Bay or Rosario Head with the gentlest downhill walk from Rosario Head.

From I-5, turn west on North Cascades Highway 20 at Exit 230 north of Mount Vernon and then turn south in about 12 miles to Deception Pass State Park.

Find both trails off Rosario Road, which branches west from Highway 20 north of the Deception Pass bridge and along the south end of Pass Lake. The road to Bowman Bay is the first one to the left; the road to Rosario Bay is the second road to the left.

From the Rosario Bay parking area, walk south through the picnic area between the boat dock on Bowman Bay and the tide pool rocks in Rosario Bay. (You may want to explore the pools at

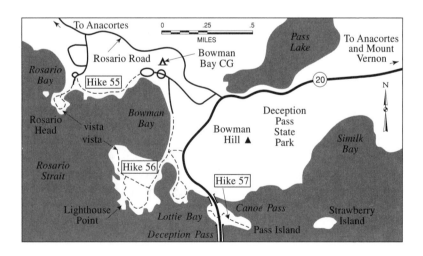

Bowman Bay

low tide here before proceeding toward Bowman Bay.)

Beyond the wood carving of the Maiden of Deception Pass (Ko-kwal-alwood), follow the trail up the left (easiest) side of the rocky crest of Rosario Head to short trails with spectacular views east into Bowman Bay, south to Whidbey Island, and west to the San Juan Islands, Rosario Strait, and the Strait of Juan de Fuca.

Keep your camera and binoculars ready to check out the screams of oystercatchers and the chatter of kingfishers working the water and rocks below. Watch, too, for an occasional seal. And flowers in the spring.

Warning: The bluff here, inviting as it is, drops steeply into rocks below.

Do not let small children stray.

Once you've run out of film or have soaked up all the scenery your memory can hold, drop back down the bluff and take the broad path east toward Bowman Bay. Views continue from informal spur paths on the edge of the bluff with a railed overlook just before the trail drops sharply to the campground on the bay.

Walk back the way you came unless you have arranged for someone to pick you up at the campground.

56 Lighthouse Point and Canoe Pass

Features: beaches, forest, vistas
One way: up to ¾ mile
Elevation gain: 100 feet
Difficulty: moderate
Open: all year
Map: Deception Pass State Park brochure

A single trail from a parking lot leads to two different places with two different views: one fork in the trail leads to vistas over a navigation light, the other to views of the spectacular Deception Pass bridge.

From I-5, turn west on North Cascades Highway 20 at Exit 230 north of Mount Vernon and then turn south in about 12 miles to Deception Pass State Park.

To reach the trail, turn right (west) off North Cascades Highway 20 just beyond Pass Lake (north of the Deception Pass bridge) onto Rosario Road and then left again on the first road to Bowman Bay. The trail starts from the parking lot on Bowman Bay before you enter Bowman Bay Campground. (See map on page 124.)

Find the path that leads to both trails near the shore of the bay beyond the boat ramp and fishing dock.

At high tide stay on the trail as it passes a small tidal marsh on the left (water birds nest here in the spring) and then switchbacks up and around the headland ahead of you before dropping back to water level on Lottie Bay and a strip of land connected to Lighthouse Point.

At low tide leave the trail, drop to the beach, and follow the shoreline to the strip of land.

To find Lighthouse Point Trail, bear west along the narrow strip of land to a path up the south side of the islandlike point.

The path leads to an exposed bluff with vistas above the navigation light out over the pass and the straits, all with wildflowers in the spring. Do *not* attempt to climb to the unmanned light. It's not only prohibited but also dangerous.

The trail continues north past the light and ends at a point overlooking Bowman Bay and down on the place from which you started. As you return take the trail to the left, completing a loop back to the shoreline strip on Lottie Bay.

To reach the Canoe Pass vista point and its view of the bridge, return to the main trail at the east end of the flat strip of land or, if on the main trail from the parking lot, continue straight ahead.

On the main trail take the first uphill fork, which climbs sharply to the vista point and then loops back down to Lottie Bay.

Deception Pass bridge from Lighthouse Point

57 Pass Island

Features: rushing tides and a classic bridge
One way: ¾ mile at most
Elevation gain: about 100 feet
Difficulty: steep and no formal trails
Open: all year
Map: Deception Pass State Park brochure

Explore a ship of rock set in a speeding tidal stream at the end of one of the most spectacular bridges in the state.

From I-5, turn west on North Cascades Highway 20 at Exit 230 north of Mount Vernon and then turn south in about 12 miles to Deception Pass State Park. (See map on page 124.)

Find a small parking area on the left as the highway curves to cross the Deception Pass bridge atop Pass Island. (If you miss it, drive across the bridge, turn back at the parking lot at the south end of the bridge, and return to the small Pass Island area just beyond a rock outcrop at the north end of the bridge.)

You'll find no formal trails here, but well-used routes lead east and west on the island. Drop from a rock outcrop east of the parking area and pick paths to the right that cross under the bridge to views back at the bridge and out over the west end of the pass. Drop straight ahead down the rocky slope to find paths leading to fishing spots at the eastern end of the island.

The views, the rushing tides, and an unusual mixture of plants make any exploration here worthwhile. Each path leads to different views of the spectacular bridge and the other islands around it. The tides rush through the pass from 9 to 14 knots—among the fastest currents near this juncture of Sound and Strait. Looking down, the rushing tide often seems to transform the island into a speeding ship.

Plants from the seashore mix with those of the mountains and others more commonly seen east of the mountains to make careful examination of what you see worthwhile.

Warning: Use care in selecting your route here. Some pitches are steep and some paths quickly disappear. All can be slippery when wet. Not for uncontrolled children, the skittish, or the unprepared. Good shoes are a must. Care and caution are essential.

Air view of Deception Pass and Pass Island

From Sand Dune Trail

58 Sand Dune Trail

Features: wetlands, dunes, beach, forest
One way: a short 1-mile loop
Elevation gain: none
Difficulty: easy
Open: all year
Map: Deception Pass State Park brochure

A sampler here, on a small scale, of all the changes in Nature—in the plants, animals, and birds—that take place, one grain of sand at a time, in every dune system up and down the coast.

Turn west on North Cascades Highway 20 at Exit 230 north of Mount Vernon and then turn south in about 12 miles to Deception Pass State Park.

From the end of the main entrance road to Deception Pass State Park, off Highway 20 south of the Deception Pass bridge, turn left on the main park road and continue to the right along the northern shore of Cranberry Lake to the large parking area near the beach.

Find Sand Dune Trail beyond the concession stand near Cranberry Lake south of the parking lot. A mural here describes the ever-changing ecological contrasts to be seen along the loop. Other displays define natural features along the way.

The paved path first leads into trees away from the hubbub of the beach and, except for the occasional sounds of jets, into a more silent world of wind, waves, and birds. Find picnic tables hidden in the trees.

The first spur trail to the left leads to a viewing platform overlooking a marsh bordering Cranberry Lake. The shallows here are swamped with willows, skunk cabbages, and cattails. Sea gulls are joined by marsh birds, hawks, and bald eagles now and then.

Back on the forest section of the trail, note the changing procession of plants. In the forest, established conifers, rhododendrons, and even scraggly looking yews stand amid bracken ferns and struggling flowers.

As the path circles toward the beach through a short moist plain behind the low row of dunes, stunted coast pines, salal, and evergreen huckleberry give way to grasses and scattered beach-adapted lupine, strawberries, tansy, and the like. And, finally, on the dunes themselves, only clumps of grass stabilize the sand.

A spur trail leads through the dunes to another overlook with views out over Rosario Strait and the Strait of Juan de Fuca. The returning section of the trail crosses more of the sparsely vegetated plain between the forest and the dunes.

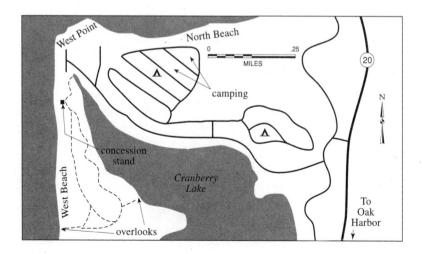

59 Anacortes Beaver Pond

Features: beaver pond and dam
One way: ¾ mile
Elevation gain: none
Difficulty: easy
Open: all year
Map: Trail Guide to Anacortes Community Forest Land

Active beaver ponds at a city's edge? In 2,200 acres of forests, wetlands, lakes, and mountaintops in a "city" forest? Believe it. And try a sample here.

Turn west to Anacortes on North Cascades Highway 20 north of Mount Vernon and follow street signs in the center of the Anacortes business district to 12th Street on the road to the Anacortes ferry terminal. From 12th Street turn south onto D Avenue and right (west) onto 31st Street, driving to the end of the short residential street. (Don't block driveways, please.)

Find the trail off the end of the street where the forest begins.

The path starts out through dense undergrowth of salal and salmonberries and brown thickets of young trees before entering a more mature forest with open sword fern groves and occasional explosions of lush yellow skunk cabbages in the spring.

At the first junction follow Trail 108 to the left (signs here

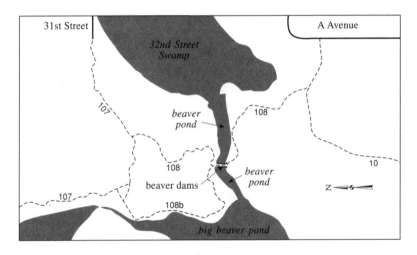

Beaver pond trail

are posted horse-high in trees), and when you cross the first stream stop. Yes, stop.

On your left, a cattail and skunk cabbage swamp where ducks explode as you approach. And on your right—look twice—a beaver dam. An old beaver dam, overgrown with grass, yes, but—if you look a second time—patched here and there with fresh sticks in newly eroded spots.

Turn back at the bridge and take Trail 108b to explore above the dam. Short way paths here lead to the top of the dam and closer views of the beavers' engineering skills. And note the tracks of deer and other creatures in muddy spots.

For fuller views of the marsh behind the dam, explore way paths off Trail 108b for about ¼ mile. Here, dead trees killed by rising water in the pond and gnawed stumps of small trees cut and carted off by beavers attest to the beavers' work.

And no, you'll probably see no beavers here, although you may now and then hear an explosive splash of water, a signal that your presence is now known. Beavers here, as elsewhere, do most of their work at night.

Return to the dam to continue on Trail 108 through more scattered old-growth cedar and Douglas fir. The trail ends at A Avenue on an old road to a nearby dump. Walk back to your car the way you came or arrange to be picked up.

60   Whistle Lake

Features: forest and lake
One way: ¾ mile
Elevation gain: slight
Difficulty: easy
Open: all year
Map: Trail Guide to Anacortes Community Forest Land

Hike past several giant, old fire-scarred Douglas fir and great, old cedar trees that survived logging at the turn of the century to a popular lake in the 2,200-acre Anacortes Community Forest.

Turn west toward Anacortes on North Cascades Highway 20 north of Mount Vernon and turn left in Anacortes on Commercial Avenue at the first T intersection as you enter town. Turn quickly left onto Fidalgo and left again at St. Mary's Catholic Church. Turn right on Hillcrest and right again on Whistle Lake Road. Jog left at the end of that road and then right following signs downhill to a parking area and trailhead, about 1.75 miles from the T intersection.

Find Gerry Wallrath Trail straight ahead at a gate off the parking area. Wallrath was an early supporter of efforts to preserve these forests for the city and left his estate to support the maintenance and development of the trail system.

You can't get lost here. Stay on the main trail, which was once a service road for what was then the city's water system. The several ancient trees define what the forest here once was.

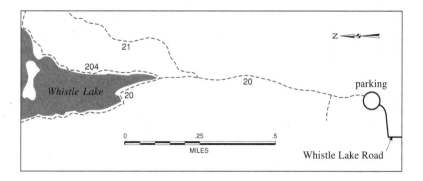

The second-growth demonstrates what it has yet to achieve before it equals that grandeur. And the mix of the two illustrates the continuity of earlier selective logging techniques. In such forests, today's great old trees were already standing when the first trees were cut. And if today's older trees were to be logged, the remaining younger trees would already be in place to fill their roles.

The trail ends at the lakeshore. Fishing, swimming, and rafting here. Experienced swimmers with local knowledge hike up the right side of the lake about ½ mile on Trail 204 to a narrow passage between the shoreline and a small island, swimming to the island where they climb a bluff and dive into the lake.

And watch for birds. Pileated woodpeckers, osprey, bald eagles, and wood ducks are common here.

Whistle Lake

61   Schriebers and Morovitz Meadows

Features: meadows and vistas
One way: 2½ miles
Elevation gain: 400 feet
Difficulty: steep in places
Open: summer
Map: Green Trails 45

From one great meadow to another with Mount Baker watching all the way, first through trees and then majestically down on open, flowered slopes.

On I-5 north of Mount Veron, turn east at Exit 230 onto North Cascades Highway 20. About 14.5 miles east of Sedro Woolley, turn north onto Baker Lake–Grandy Lake Road (or the road to Baker Lake, depending on the sign you read) and reach the boundary of Mount Baker–Snoqualmie National Forest (it's signed) in about 12 miles.

To find the trail turn left (west) off Baker Lake Road just inside the forest boundary onto Forest Road 12 and then, in 3.5 miles, onto Road 13. Find the trailhead in 5 more miles off a well-developed parking area, to the left, beside the toilets.

The trail in the first mile to Schriebers Meadow wanders

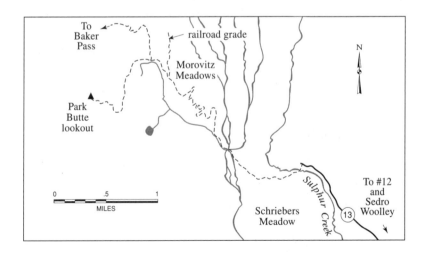

Morovitz Meadows and Mount Baker

through increasingly open timber past occasional small ponds, each with its own reflected glimpse of Mount Baker. Other clearings and small patches of trees with still more ponds and sinkholes beckon everywhere.

(Swarms of mosquitoes here most summers, but bugless in the fall when the meadows turn rich with berries and color.)

At the end of the mile, the trail passes the site of a former shelter and crosses streams from Easton Glacier before its steep switchback climb to the more open Morovitz Meadows at 4,700 feet with still more views and places begging to be explored.

At the meadows, it is impossible to say which way to turn. One ridge may look down on a whole city of marmots, another out on a flower slope. The next may feature wind-sculptured trees. Another, snarls of rock. But over all of them, no matter which you choose, your host, proud and stately Mount Baker.

Other trails—all uphill—continue on to the Railroad Grade (4,900 feet), Baker Pass (5,000 feet), and Park Butte Lookout (5,400 feet). And each is worth the trip.

Mount Baker from Dock Butte

62 Blue Lake and Dock Butte

Features: lake, meadows, vistas
One way: Blue Lake, ¾ mile; Dock Butte, 1 mile
Elevation gain: Blue Lake, 100 feet; Dock Butte, 700 feet
Difficulty: steep in places
Open: summer
Map: Green Trails 45

Two destinations and two trails here, really. Each worth a visit all its own. But both are so closely linked that to hike to one without visiting the other would be a waste of effort.

On I-5 north of Mount Vernon, turn east at Exit 230 onto North Cascades Highway 20. About 14.5 miles east of Sedro Woolley, turn north onto Baker Lake–Grandy Lake Road (or the road to Baker Lake, depending on the sign you read) and reach the boundary of Mount Baker–Snoqualmie National Forest (it's signed) in about 12 miles.

To find the trail turn left (west) off Baker Lake Road just inside the forest boundary onto Forest Road 12. In 7 miles turn left onto Road 1230, driving another 4 miles to the end of the road (with views of Baker, Shuksan, Blum, and other North Cascades peaks in the last 3 miles).

At the end of the road, the trail climbs a slight ridge ⅓ mile to a junction: Dock Butte Trail to the right, Blue Lake Trail to the left. Dock Butte Trail climbs steadily up a series of switchbacks with increasing views toward Mount Baker, reaching an open meadow at about 4,700 feet—with flowers in the summer, colors in the fall—atop a beautiful alpine plateau.

Follow the trail south past pleasant pools, gray outcrops of rock, overgrown mine prospects, weathered trees, and camping spots. Views swing here from the Twin Sisters in the east, to Baker and Shuksan, up the Baker River valley to the Pickets, and westward to Blum, Hagan, and Bacon.

Wander here certainly before returning to the lake. And, if you choose, climb a rugged and very steep path another ½ mile and up another 500 feet in elevation to the top of the pointed butte and the former Dock Butte lookout site at 5,200 feet. Not for the queasy. Add Mount Rainier here to your list of peaks.

On the way down, turn right downhill at the trail junction to visit Blue Lake. The soggy path drops downhill through timber to a 13-acre lake at 4,000 feet. Talus slopes rise at the far end. Meadows surround the rest.

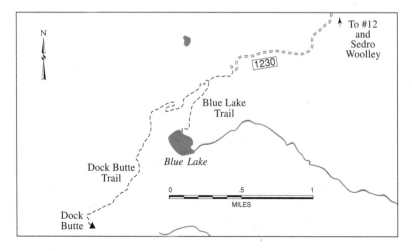

63   Shadow of Sentinels

Features: old-growth forest
One way: ½-mile loop
Elevation gain: none
Difficulty: wheelchair trail
Open: spring to winter
Map: Green Trails 46

Find here all the reasons ever needed for preserving what's left of old-growth forests in western Washington. All from one lush, short, and easy trail.

On I-5 north of Mount Vernon, turn east at Exit 230 onto North Cascades Highway 20. About 14.5 miles east of Sedro Woolley, turn north onto Baker Lake–Grandy Lake Road (or the road to Baker Lake, depending on the sign you read) and reach the boundary of Mount Baker–Snoqualmie National Forest (it's signed) in about 12 miles.

From the boundary, continue on Baker Lake Road (now Forest Road 11) about 3.5 miles, finding the nature trail on the right about 0.75 mile beyond the Koma Kulshan Guard Station.

You'll find the best of every ancient forest here on this one short loop. Huge Douglas firs and hemlocks, some more than 600 years old, tower high above a still-evolving, multilayered canopy of younger trees that rise over, and from, other rotting giants toppled by time and winds.

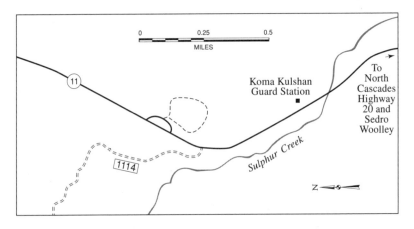

Shadow of Sentinels Nature Trail

Not a trail to rush through, no, for this old forest is more than trees. Admire the mosses, the variety of ferns, the scraps of lichens on the trail, and the change of wild flowers (a new display for every week). And listen to the croak of frogs, the trill of wrens, the thrush's scale of single notes, the drum of woodpeckers on rotting snags, and even the robin's call.

Bring your camera, binoculars, bird and flower books, for you'll find here—if you take the time to look—what you'll find in most west-slope, old-growth forests everywhere, assuring you, in saying that, that every forest grove is different and that having seen one you've not seen all. An excellent sample here. No more.

64 Upper Baker River

Features: river and forest
One way: 1½ miles or less
Elevation gain: 200 feet
Difficulty: moderate
Open: spring to fall
Map: Green Trails 14

A mountain river here, wild, fresh, and untrammeled, flowing from the North Cascades. Along the upper Baker River on a short trail almost as wild. With occasional surprise views of surrounding peaks.

On I-5 north of Mount Vernon, turn east at Exit 230 onto North Cascades Highway 20. About 14.5 miles east of Sedro Woolley, turn north onto Baker Lake–Grandy Lake Road (or the road to Baker Lake, depending on the sign you read) and reach the boundary of Mount Baker–Snoqualmie National Forest (it's signed) in about 12 miles.

From the boundary, continue on Baker Lake Road (now Forest Road 11), with views of Mount Baker all along the way, to its end, and then turn left on Spur Road 1168 with a parking lot and trailhead at its end, about 14.5 miles from the boundary.

The trail starts down a long-abandoned logging spur away

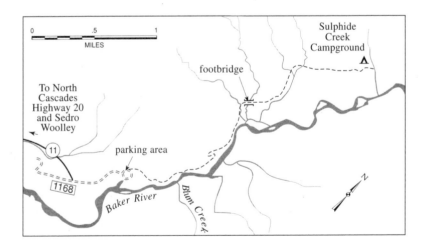

Sulphide Creek

from the river off the upstream side of the parking lot. In less than ¼ mile, the spur ends and the trail enters a cluster of grand old cedar trees that seem to have outlived everything around them and then winds around huge boulders, under arches of moss-draped vine maples and across several short log bridges.

Watch for indications of a beaver pond through the trees and undergrowth on your left. Old alders stand by themselves in the middle of the water. No approach to the ponds.

Take time to visit every cove along the river and explore every sandbar and gravel bar. And note, too, how the river continues to shape the valley as its sweeps back and forth on an ever-changing course, adding shoreline here, destroying it there.

Wild salmon once spawned here. Now, returning salmon have to be trucked from Concrete to spawning grounds above the dam.

In about a mile the trail climbs around a rocky point and then drops away from the river across a brushy flat, reaching the boundary of North Cascades National Park at 1¾ miles.

The trail ends in another ¾ mile at a small campground on Sulphide Creek. Backcountry permits are required for camping there.

Mount Baker reflected in Baker Lake

65 East Bank

Features: forest, lake, vistas
One way: 2 miles
Elevation loss: 300 feet
Difficulty: moderate
Open: spring to winter
Map: Green Trails 46

First, a forest logged once selectively and almost as rich now as it was then. Then, Baker Lake, with explosive views of its namesake peak.

On I-5 north of Mount Vernon, turn east at Exit 230 onto North Cascades Highway 20. About 14.5 miles east of Sedro Woolley, turn north onto Baker Lake–Grandy Lake Road (or the road to Baker Lake, depending on the sign you read) and reach the boundary of Mount Baker–Snoqualmie National Forest (it's signed) in about 12 miles.

Continue north on what has now become Forest Road 11. Turn right onto Road 1106 to cross the top of Upper Baker Dam, and then follow Road 1107 around to the left (toward Anderson and Watson lakes).

Find the East Bank trailhead in little more than 0.5 mile, off a parking strip on the left.

The path drops immediately into forest and then crosses three little creeks before leveling out a little in older forest.

Note the huge old stumps here, hand-logged by men who stood on springboards jammed into the side of the tree in the early part of the century.

The forest here is probably as open now as it was when the huge trees were first cut down. Most of the large trees standing now were no doubt well established when the much larger trees were felled. (Some of today's big Douglas fir could never have attained their size in 90 years.)

The path, which now sometimes goes up while going down, climbs over the toe of a ridge, drops, and climbs again before dropping down to a large log bridge over noisy Anderson Creek.

Views now of Mount Baker from a beach on a small cove and sand spit at the end of a short unmarked path downhill to the left at the start of the bridge.

Beyond the bridge in ¼ mile more or less, take a more developed spur trail to the left, which drops for ¼ mile down a neck of land to the lake with even better views.

Stop here, or return to the main trail and go on to Maple Grove Camp, largely for fishermen and boaters, at the end of the main trail in another 2 miles.

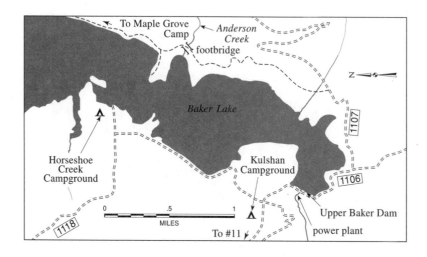

66   Anderson and Watson Lakes

Features: mountain lakes and a lookout, too
One way: 1½–2½ miles
Elevation gain: 500–1,200 feet
Difficulty: steep to very steep
Open: summer
Map: Green Trails 46

Two clusters of alpine lakes at 4,500 feet in spectacular meadow country plus an even higher (at 5,400 feet) former lookout site with views almost everywhere, all from the end of a high and scenic, but sometimes poorly maintained, forest road.

On I-5 north of Mount Vernon, turn east at Exit 230 onto North Cascades Highway 20. About 14.5 miles east of Sedro Woolley, turn north onto Baker Lake–Grandy Lake Road (or the road to Baker Lake, depending on the sign you read) and reach the boundary of Mount Baker–Snoqualmie National Forest (it's signed) in about 12 miles.

Continue north on what has now become Forest Road 11, turn right onto Road 1106 to cross the top of Upper Baker Dam, and then follow Road 1107 around to the left. Find trailhead parking in another 10.5 miles.

The trail to both clusters of lakes and to the lookout starts

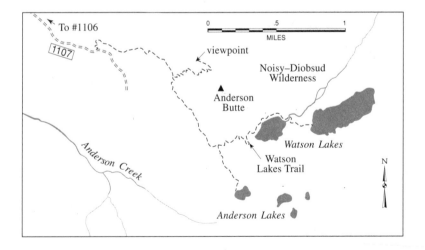

Watson Lake

sharply from the parking area, climbing briskly the first mile to the junction with Anderson Butte Trail, on another long half mile to the junction with Watson Lakes Trail, and a final half-plus mile to Anderson Lakes.

From the main trail the path to the lookout site on Anderson Butte switchbacks up persistently and often steeply 700 feet in ½ mile to a boulder outcrop on the edge of the Noisy–Diobsud Wilderness with awesome views of Mounts Baker and Shuksan and other Cascades peaks to the south. No views of the lakes.

From the main trail to Watson Lakes, the path climbs steeply uphill to the left over a ridge into the Noisy–Diobsud Wilderness before dropping to the two big Watson Lakes. Views over both from a steep meadow before you reach the lakes. (A trail along the left side of the first lake leads to the second.)

The main trail, which continues to the first of the Anderson Lakes, drops gradually through meadows from the Watson Lakes turnoff. Bear right at the first lake for a breathtaking look of Mount Baker from a pretty meadow just across the creek. No formal trail to two other lakes that lie about 500 feet higher atop the ridge to the left (east).

Camping at Watson Lakes near the first lake or on meadows between the two lakes. Camping also near Anderson Lake.

Spend a day at either one or a weekend at both.

67 Sauk Mountain

Features: steep meadows and grand vistas
One way: 2-plus miles
Elevation gain: 1,200 feet
Difficulty: steep
Open: summer
Map: Green Trails 46

Great views of the Sauk, Skagit, and Cascade river valleys from the end of a zigzag forest road to the trail parking lot with a spectacle of peaks from an old lookout site at 5,537 feet.

On I-5 north of Mount Vernon, turn east at Exit 230 onto North Cascades Highway 20 and drive to Concrete. In about another 10 miles, turn north (left) on easy-to-miss Forest Road 1030 along the western boundary of Rockport State Park (about 1.5 miles west of the junction of Highways 20 and 530 in Rockport).

Skagit River from Sauk Mountain trail

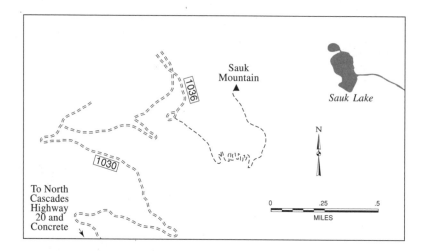

Forest Road 1030 switchbacks a low-gear 7 miles to a junction (right) with short Spur Road 1036. Turn right to turnaround parking with the grand overlook in a few hundred yards at the end of the spur.

Find the trail to the top of Sauk Mountain off the east side of the parking area. It drops slightly at the start but then begins a steady switchback climb across steep meadows to the ridgetop and lookout site.

No one seems to agree on the number of switchbacks on this trail. Some say twenty-six, others twenty-eight, and still others twenty-nine. But the truth is, it doesn't really matter. First, because most of them are short, and, second, because the demanding, ever-changing vistas and spectacular flower meadows make counting impossible anyway.

At the ridge, a spur path branches right and drops down, about as far as you have climbed, to Sauk Lake. Most hikers pass up the opportunity and continue ahead to the lookout site in a less-steep and long ½ mile to fantastic vistas of Glacier Peak; Mounts Baker, Shuksan, Whitehorse, White Chuck, and Pugh; and, on clear days, Mount Rainier, Puget Sound, and the San Juan Islands.

Warning: Use care here. Do not shortcut switchbacks or dislodge rocks. And warn those who do that they are endangering the lives of those on the trail below them.

Slide Lake

68 Slide Lake

Features: forest and lake with supporting ponds
One way: 1¼ miles
Elevation gain: 300 feet
Difficulty: moderate
Open: summer
Map: Green Trails 79

Surprising ponds and a spectacular lake, tucked in a mountain bowl, at the end of a short trail filled with moss-covered boulders and other surprises.

On I-5 north of Mount Vernon, turn east at Exit 230 onto North Cascades Highway 20 and drive to Rockport. From Rockport drive south on Rockport–Darrington Highway 530, and turn

east (left) in 1.9 miles onto Illabot Creek Forest Road 16. Drive
to the Otter Creek trailhead in 20 miles.

The path to Slide Lake wanders through a cool, shady
tumble of old boulders topped with huge, ancient hemlocks. Don't
hurry. Nature worked a long time to create this scene, so soak up
all of the visual surprises as you go. Forest flowers, huckleberries, salmonberries, and gooseberries in season.

The trail enters the Glacier Peak Wilderness at the end of a
mile, skirts several ponds, and reaches the main lake (3,300 feet)
with the best vistas in ¼ mile more.

Camp and picnic places at the end of the trail along with
views up at Snowking Mountain. And treat the area with care: it
has been heavily used over time, as you can see. Without your
consideration it could still be destroyed.

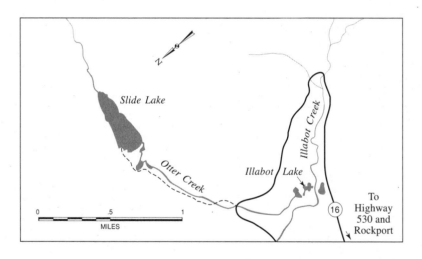

69 Kindy Creek Trail

Features: rich forest
One way: 1 mile plus
Elevation gain: about 200 feet
Difficulty: moderate
Open: summer
Map: trail not shown on forest or Green Trail maps

A rich, grand grove of ancient hemlock, cedar, and Douglas fir on an unmarked trail that you, at least, will not forget. Most of the time, you'll be the only hiker (or hikers) here.

On I-5 north of Mount Vernon, turn east at Exit 230 onto North Cascades Highway 20 and continue to Marblemount. From Marblemount continue east across the Skagit River on Cascade River Road 15.

About 6 miles beyond Marble Creek Campground, turn sharply south (right) just beyond the 13-mile marker onto Road 1570. (Watch for a wide turnout on the left side of the road where big trucks swing wide off the spur.)

Follow Road 1570 downhill, keeping straight ahead at the first fork, crossing the Cascade River in about 1.6 miles, and turning left on the far side of the bridge.

In about 0.3 mile, turn left onto Road 1571, driving to the

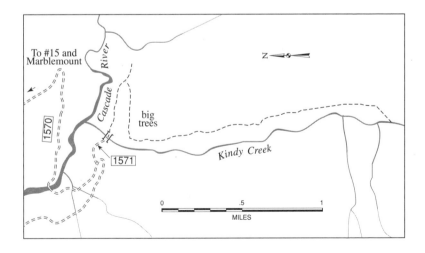

Tall trees on Kindy Creek trail

end of the road at a rotting bridge across Kindy Creek.

Walk across the bridge over this startling, clear creek and follow an old logging track to a wide point where the road once turned uphill. (Avoid the inviting game trails that climb steeply across sandy slopes to your right.)

The old road ends and the real Kindy Creek trail begins at an unused trail board in another 100 yards or less.

The trail, now a pleasant path, climbs gradually back toward Kindy Creek through everything you'd expect to see in an open, untouched forest with towering trees up to 8 feet in diameter.

As spring and summer pass: star flowers and queen cups, through bunchberries and pipsissewas, to huckleberries and even salal amid colored vine maples into the fall.

The path crests at about 1,500 feet before dropping down and ending in a washout on Kindy Creek, well above the place you started. Return the way you came, taking time to note all the beauties you may have missed.

70 Cascade Pass

Features: mountain spectacles of every sort
One way: 3¾ miles
Elevation gain: 1,800 feet
Difficulty: steep
Open: midsummer
Map: Green Trails 80

The queen of all short Cascade mountain hikes. Longer, yes, than most of the others listed here. But you'll forget the added effort in the spectacle of glaciers, peaks, flowers, and vistas that surround you everywhere.

On I-5 north of Mount Vernon, turn east at Exit 230 onto North Cascades Highway 20 and continue to Marblemount. From Marblemount continue east across the Skagit River on Cascade River Road 15 and drive 25 miles to a parking area at the end of the road in North Cascades National Park.

The grandeur here begins before you even leave your car at 3,600 feet. From just the parking area: glaciers on Johannesburg Mountain to the southwest and Cascade Pass above you to the east.

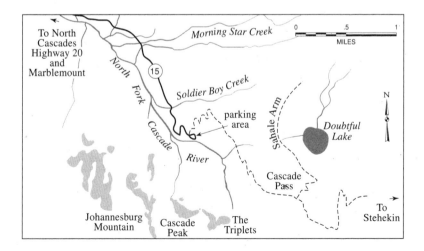

Eldorado Peak, left, *and Boston Basin,* right, *from small tarn near Cascade Pass*

The trail to Cascade Pass from the parking lot switchbacks very gradually through trees, topping out at last on a long traverse up to the pass (5,400 feet) across alpine meadows with vistas, yes, but closer up paintbrush, monkey flower, penstemon, and whole hillsides of red columbine, to just begin the list of flowers.

At the pass, whistling marmots, certainly. Pikas scurrying in the rocks. But most of all, glaciers everywhere with avalanches crashing from their hanging cliffs of ice.

And views to the east out over the Stehekin Valley.

If you have time, walk the switchback path just beyond the crest uphill to the left toward Sahale Arm for even more exciting vistas. Another mile and 800 feet will take you to a ridge overlooking Doubtful Lake and still broader views of the towering peaks around you.

No camping permitted at the pass, and hikers are urged to stay on the trail. Heavy use here in the past almost destroyed this area for good.

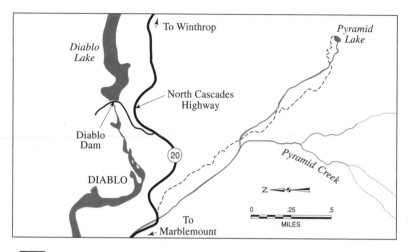

71 Pyramid Lake

Features: forest and tiny lake
One way: a long 2 miles
Elevation gain: 1,500 feet
Difficulty: very steep
Open: summer
Map: Green Trails 48

Peculiarly, this is a very popular trail. You'll find smiling adults and children working their way up and down almost any day or time of day all summer long. But if you've hiked other trails, almost anywhere in this region, you'll have to wonder why.

First, it's steep beyond belief. The lake at the end is almost small enough to spit across. And the forest, for the first third, at least, is the scrawniest and most unattractive in this entire book.

So why the many who struggle here? Who knows. You'll have to hike and judge it for yourself.

On I-5 north of Mount Vernon, turn east at Exit 230 onto North Cascades Highway 20 and continue through Marblemount to the Seattle City Light community of Newhalem.

Find the trail to the lake about 6.5 miles east of Newhalem (3.4 miles west of Colonial Creek Campground) with parking on the north (lake) side of the highway. The trail is uphill across the road in a gully.

The rocky path grinds up through an old burn now grown with scrawny lodgepole pine past an occasional old Douglas fir scarred, but not destroyed, by fire.

After maybe a 700-foot gain in elevation and a glimpse of Pyramid Peak through the trees, the path wanders (briefly) through a grove of old cedars and fir before climbing again in short, steep spurts over roots and rocks—up 100 feet here and 200 feet there—through still more small groves (note occasional old blazes on the trees) until—voila!—at 2,600 feet the lake. A pond. A puddle. The end. With barely a place to sit and rest. With a glimpse—no more—of Pyramid Peak above the trees. All may not be lost, however. Sundews, small insect-eating plants, have been noted on logs floating in this small pond. And if you find one, leave it be.

And oh, yes. Return the way you came, finding it just as steep going down as it was when you struggled up.

Pyramid Peak from Pyramid Lake

72 Thunder Creek

Features: rich forest, flowers, creek
One way: 2 miles or less
Elevation gain: 300 feet
Difficulty: easy to moderate
Open: summer
Map: Green Trails 48

From one path here, two destinations: a pleasant, level river walk up Thunder Creek and a generous sample of a mountain forest on the Thunder Woods Nature Trail. Both are worth the walk.

On I-5 north of Mount Vernon, turn east at Exit 230 onto North Cascades Highway 20 and continue to Marblemount. From Marblemount drive north 24 miles to Colonial Creek Campground on Thunder Arm in North Cascades National Park.

Find the start of both these hikes behind the amphitheater at the far end of the loop in the southern, upriver, half of the campground.

Thunder Woods Nature Trail. Find the short-mile-long trail uphill at a display sign about ¼ mile from the amphitheater. The path here loops up through almost every type of natural setting to be found in old-growth, unlogged forests in this park: ancient cedars straddle boulders, towering Douglas firs perch on stilts

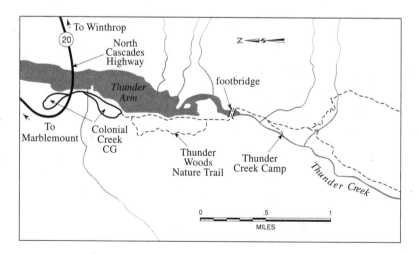

Thunder Creek Trail

above the rotting logs they sprouted on, and old giants sprawl across the forest floor, their uptilted root fans decked with ferns, while the rotting trunks of others sprout seedling trees.

The trail, like all good forest trails, climbs here, drops there, struggles over roots and rocks and even crosses a slope of scree. Most often, though, it winds gently through a silence that pervades ancient forests everywhere.

After climbing about 300 feet past all of the numbered stations explained in the park brochure, the path drops to the main trail: turn left to camp or right down Thunder Arm again.

Thunder Creek Trail. From the campground, this trail winds on above Thunder Arm more than ¾ mile and then crosses a suspension bridge over Thunder Creek to continue through lush forest to a spur (right) to Thunder Creek Camp near the creek about 2 miles from the campground.

Technically, there's no "rain forest" here, yet the green abundance of trees and plants along this trail gives a richness to the forest that deserves that name. Great trees, vine maples arched with moss, moss-cushioned logs, flowers in every season. Don't hurry here. Look carefully and see.

73 Ross Dam

Features: small waterfalls, great boulders, huge power dam
One way: less than a mile
Elevation change: 500 feet down, 500 feet back up
Difficulty: moderate to steep
Open: spring to fall
Map: Green Trails 48

More here than a hydroelectric power dam and a backwater lake that stretches north into Canada: a contrasting mixture, too, of Nature's tranquility and violence.

On I-5 north of Mount Vernon, turn east at Exit 230 onto North Cascades Highway 20 and continue to Marblemount. From Marblemount drive north 24 miles to Colonial Creek Campground on Thunder Arm in North Cascades National Park.

Find the trailhead about 4 miles beyond the campground off a parking area on the left (north) side of the highway at 2,800 feet.

The path, off the left side of the parking area, drops down to a wooden bridge over cascading Happy Creek and a resting place between two small tumbling waterfalls. A tranquil destination of its own. (In another 50 yards or so, the trail affords a better view back at this small gorge and waterfall.)

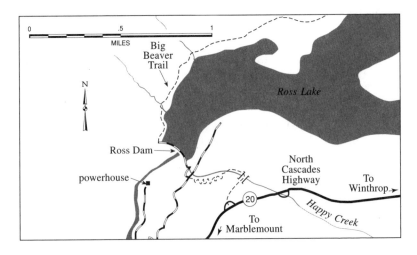

Ross Dam

Farther down, the path passes a huge slab of rock that toppled off some higher cliff and jammed itself into the gorge. As you pass this now-passive sign of violence, watch for a way path to the left with a glimpse of still another waterfall.

Shortly, the path starts a series of switchbacks down to a building perched on a bluff and the first full view down on the dam and out at the mountains. (Note here how a trail below follows the lakeshore to the right from the far side of the dam toward Beaver Creek and beyond.)

Still more switchbacks now lead down to a road to the right that goes to the top of the dam and to the left that drops sharply to the powerhouse on Diablo Lake and the beginning of a trail there that winds west to the top of Diablo Dam. And, yes, of course, you can also walk across the dam and look down on its honeycombed concrete face.

And bear in mind before you start, on hot days certainly: Hikers that hike down here must also hike back up.

74 Canyon Creek

Features: forest, streams, history
One way: less than 1 mile
Elevation gain: none
Difficulty: easy
Open: summer
Map: Green Trails 49

Two creeks, two bridges, through lovely open forest to a place where two men 90 years ago, without roads or trails or bridges, decided to build their "home."

From the west, on I-5 north of Mount Vernon, turn east at Exit 230 onto North Cascades Highway 20 and continue to Marblemount. From Marblemount drive 32.8 miles to a trailhead off a parking area on Canyon Creek just below the highway on the left. From the east, drive from Winthrop west 55.1 miles.

The trail drops off the upriver end of the parking lot into a lovely forest bench curving right to a bridge supported on sacks filled with concrete over Granite Creek.

Follow the low, level path down the creek now to a house and then across a bridge over Canyon Creek. The trail to the left there leads to a Forest Service barn that once housed mules and horses used to patrol this pristine area before the highway was built.

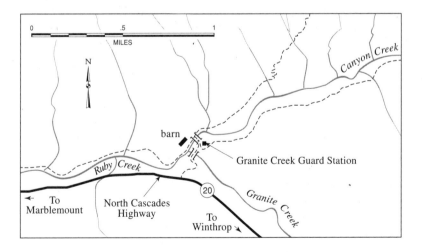

Historic cabin along Canyon Creek

According to historians, the first cabin at the pleasant junction of these two creeks was built in 1902 by two sailors who were looking for gold. Twenty years later another prospector moved the house, one log at a time, to where it now stands. It was used as a Forest Service backcountry guard station for more than 20 years.

This is a beautiful area. And it's plain why it served so long as someone's home. So treat all you find here with respect and care. Why destroy what was so difficult to build? Why desecrate such a pleasant place?

As someone else said: Have a little respect for history. And for the beauty that drew men here, even in a search for gold.

75 Rainy Lake

Features: classic high-mountain lake
One way: 1 mile
Elevation gain: very slight
Difficulty: easy (for wheelchairs)
Open: summer
Map: Green Trails 50

A perfect mountain lake at 4,800 feet—with waterfalls from a glacier even—at the end of a paved mile-long trail through lovely subalpine forest.

On I-5 north of Mount Vernon, turn east at Exit 230 onto North Cascades Highway 20 and continue to Marblemount. From Marblemount drive another 51 miles to Rainy Pass and a signed parking and picnic area south (to the right) of the highway.

Find the paved trail off the entrance (east) end of the parking loop.

This path, paved as it is, is part of the forest here, hugging the natural contours of the slopes without any great engineering cuts or fills through a forest of Engelmann spruce and Douglas fir. With flower surprises everywhere: monkey flowers soaking their roots in wet spots here and there with paintbrushes, spring beauties, and foam flowers occurring everywhere.

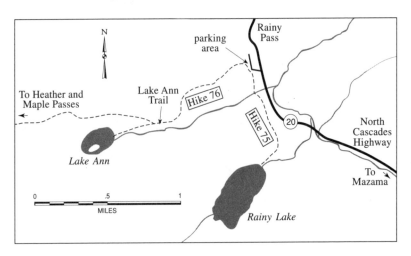

Rainy Lake

Even highway noises that reach the trail are drowned out by occasional small tumbling streams. Cool breezes brush the trail as you approach the lake, and downhill through the trees you can see a portion of the Pacific Crest Trail as it makes its way east and then south to Lake Chelan.

At the lake find a viewing platform with benches but, more important, a vista filled with not-so-distant mountain ledges, terraces, snow, rock, and waterfalls below Lyall Glacier, itself tucked into the side of Frisco Mountain.

Don't, however, expect to enjoy this scenery alone. Visitors of every shape and form, in street shoes, sandals, even barefoot, in shorts, dresses, even bathing suits, walk this mile—as well they should—to see and take pictures of this rare scene.

76 Lake Ann

Features: forests, lake, meadows
One way: 2 miles
Elevation gain: 700 feet
Difficulty: moderate to steep
Open: midsummer
Maps: Green Trails 49, 50

A pretty alpine lake with its own island and downstream ponds. And beyond, if you have the time and energy, higher alpine heather ridges with marmots, flowers, and vistas.

On I-5 north of Mount Vernon, turn east at Exit 230 onto North Cascades Highway 20 and continue to Marblemount. From Marblemount drive another 51 miles to Rainy Pass and a signed parking and picnic area south (to the right) of the highway. (See map on page 164.)

Find the trail uphill to the right, off the entrance (east) end of the parking loop. It's signed.

The path to Lake Ann and beyond climbs easily the first 1½ miles to a junction: Lake Ann left, Heather and Maple passes to the right.

Beyond the junction, Lake Ann Trail wends another half mile around ponds and marshes, all worth strolling through, to the lake at 5,475 feet in a snow-fringed cirque with better vistas still. Marsh-loving flowers everywhere.

The trail to the right climbs to views down on the lake before switchbacking to Heather Pass, a meadow-covered place at about 6,200 feet with limited vistas to the north.

After a traverse to the south, the trail then climbs to Maple Pass (6,600 feet) at the end of 3-plus miles, with still more meadows, marmots, and the most spectacular views of all. On clear weekends watch for climbers on surrounding, nearby peaks. You'll often hear them talking before you see them in the rocks.

Lake Ann

77 Blue Lake

Features: high lake, meadows, peaks
One way: 2¼ miles
Elevation gain: about 1,100 feet
Difficulty: moderate
Open: midsummer
Map: Green Trails 50

Look up at the cliffs of Liberty Bell and Early Winters Spires and north at Cutthroat Peak from the shores of a rock-rimmed mountain lake.

On I-5 north of Mount Vernon, turn east at Exit 230 onto North Cascades Highway 20 and continue to Marblemount. From Marblemount drive another 55 miles to a trailhead about 3 miles beyond Rainy Pass.

Find the trail off a parking area at the end of a short spur road to the right (south) of the highway.

The trail makes its way upward parallel to the highway for a long ¼ mile before switchbacking away from the noisy road.

At the end of a long mile, the path climbs into an avalanche meadow with views and in another ½ mile crosses a steep flower-covered meadow with still greater views below the towering crags of Liberty Bell. Note a mountain climbers' path to the left.

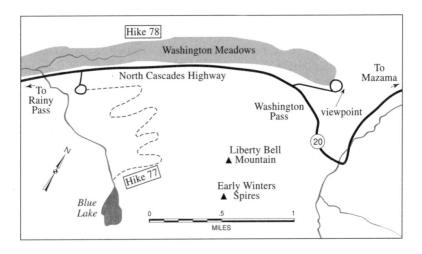

Blue Lake

The trail reaches the outlet of the lake at 6,300 feet. A rock outcrop provides a picnic, resting, and viewing spot near an abandoned shelter. There's no formal trail around the lake. Take time, however, to explore the ridge to the right of the lake with its pretty ponds and larches that glow golden in the fall.

No highway noises here, but on weekends listen for the calls of climbers on Liberty Bell and Early Winters Spires.

78 Washington Meadows

Features: high, lush meadows and Liberty Bell Mountain
One way: set your own limit
Elevation gain: none
Difficulty: soggy
Open: midsummer
Map: Green Trails 50

The flowers and vistas here belong to the meadow at 5,500 feet. But the discoveries belong to you.

On I-5 north of Mount Vernon, turn east at Exit 230 onto North Cascades Highway 20 and continue to Marblemount and then on to Washington Pass. (See map on page 168.)

Find this meadow on the west (left) side of the entry road to Washington Pass Overlook. Park on the west side of the road (after you've visited the overlook, of course) and pick your own short path to the meadow.

You'll find no formal trails, although the Pacific Crest Trail crossed the meadows before the highway was constructed.

Unmarked paths below the road that start and then stop lead to meadow corners you'll be unable to resist, with views up at Liberty Bell—the peak that commands this place—that change with each new little creek, pond, and tree.

Two suggestions, though, to start. First, be prepared for mosquitoes, tons of them, unless it's a breezy day. And second, this is a soggy place. In late fall you may be able to wander without getting your feet wet, but most of the time some sort of waterproof or rubber shoes will help.

Sometime-paths on the south and east side of the meadow below the highway and entrance road are most likely to remain above the marshy waterline. Watch for deer tracks here and perhaps even tracks of bear. And in the small ponds, frogs for sure, and in the streams, if you're lucky, the flash of a fleeing trout.

But it is the meadow flowers that command the most attention in these meadows. Nature changes her bouquets here almost every week.

It would be pointless to try and list all the flowers. Cotton grass for sure. Gentians in the fall. Bog orchids and elephant head without fail. You'll need a flower book to help complete your list. And on warm days, note, too, the sweet smell of alpine fir.

Take nothing and destroy nothing as you walk here. Look only, so others can enjoy. Tenderly is the rule, and fragile, oh so fragile, is the reason why.

And as you leave? Bow deeply to the mountain and applaud.

Liberty Bell from Washington Meadows

79 Cutthroat Lake

Features: alpine lake
One way: 2 miles
Elevation gain: 450 feet
Difficulty: moderate
Open: midsummer
Map: Green Trails 50

As cars parked at the trailhead often indicate: This is a popular place. But take heart, many hikers use this as a jumping-off place for treks beyond the lake into the North Cascades.

From the west, drive east on North Cascades Highway 20, finding the trailhead at the end of uphill Spur Road 400 about 4.6 miles beyond Washington Pass. Or from Winthrop, drive about 1.5 miles beyond Lone Fir Campground. (Even the view from Road 400 is worth the trip.)

The trail starts in a heavily used sandy flat and then climbs gradually away from the creek to a junction in 1¾ miles. (The uphill trail to the right climbs sharply here to Cutthroat Pass in almost 4 miles. A shorter trip offers views down on the lake.)

The path left drops to the lake tucked into a circle of mountains at 4,935 feet in a short quarter mile. Picnic spots, flowers in their season, and endless views.

No camping within 200 feet of the lake.

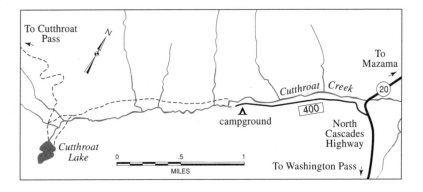

Cutthroat Lake

80 Cedar Falls

Features: waterfalls
One way: 1¾ miles
Elevation gain: slight
Difficulty: easy, but slick rocks at falls
Open: spring
Map: Green Trails 51

Walk above noisy Cedar Creek to a tumble of waterfalls with resting places and views from slabs of rocks above the falls. A must for any falls collector.

From the west, drive east on North Cascades Highway 20 over Washington Pass to Klipchuck Campground, about 70 miles from Marblemount. From the east drive 18 miles west of Winthrop.

About 0.3 mile beyond the campground, turn right (east) on Spur Road 200 (the road is signed "Trailhead" on the highway). Drive about 0.9 mile to a gravel pit, and find the trail uphill off the creek side of the pit.

The path climbs gradually above Cedar Creek through an open sidehill forest of fir and spruce with occasional stands of cedar.

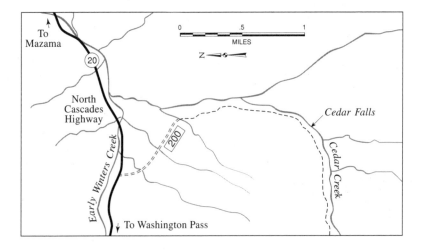

You'll hear the waterfalls before you see them. Water here tumbles 50 feet or more in a series of falls from several crystal pools.

Warning: Wet rocks can be slippery here, and there are no fences or barriers. So pick your way with care on all of the steep sidehills and slopes around and above the falls. Not for uncontrolled children.

Cedar Falls

81 Goat Peak Lookout

Features: vistas, vistas, vistas
One way: 2½ miles
Elevation gain: 1,400 feet
Difficulty: moderate to steep
Open: midsummer
Map: Green Trails 51

Walk to absolutely the most spectacular views in this entire area from a lookout atop Goat Peak at 7,000 feet that you can see from practically every highway in the valley.

From the west, drive east on North Cascades Highway 20 over Rainy and Washington passes into the Methow Valley. Turn north (left) off the highway to Mazama, less than 2 miles east of the Early Winters Information Center.

Turn right at Mazama onto Mazama/Harts Pass/Lost River Road (depending on the map you use) and then sharply left uphill in about 2 miles onto Forest Road 52. (From the east, drive west from Winthrop on Highway 20 and turn right just before the highway crosses the Methow River in about 8 miles. Turn right again in 3.4 miles onto Forest Road 52.)

In 2.2 miles (on Road 52), turn left onto Road 5225. In 3.3

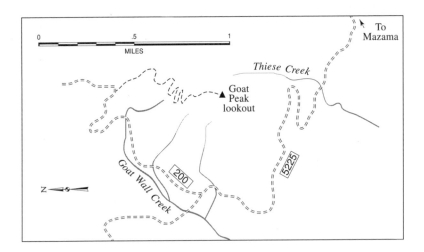

Goat Peak Lookout

miles (great vistas here), turn right onto Spur Road 5225-200, driving to the trailhead on the right in another 2.5 miles.

The trail starts out on a ridge, climbing alternately through meadows and open forest. In about 1 mile it settles down to the serious work of gaining elevation, topping out on the ridge to wander up and down then through vistas and wildflowers, naturally, to the lookout perched on the valley rim.

And from the lookout? Peaks everywhere. To the south, all of the Methow Valley and the North Cascades Highway, Silver Star Mountain with its glaciers, and Gardner Mountain to its left, plus, to the east, peaks of the Cascade Crest and, to the north and west, mountains within the Pasayten Wilderness.

82   Slate Peak and High Meadows

Features: alpine meadows and views plus views
One way: 2 miles or more
Elevation gain: 200 feet
Difficulty: easy
Open: midsummer
Maps: Green Trails 18, 50

Two choices here, and pick them both.

The first leads through high meadows on the Pacific Crest Trail. The other to sweeping vistas from the top of Slate Peak at 7,440 feet.

From the west, drive east on North Cascades Highway 20 over Rainy and Washington passes into the Methow Valley and turn north (left) off the highway to Mazama, less than 2 miles east of the Early Winters Information Center.

Turn left in Mazama and follow the narrow and steep Harts Pass Road 5400 for 18.5 miles to Harts Pass. At the pass turn north on Spur Road 600.

To hike through the high meadows along the Pacific Crest Trail, find the trailhead to the left at 6,600 feet off a hairpin turn in Spur Road 600 in about 1.5 miles.

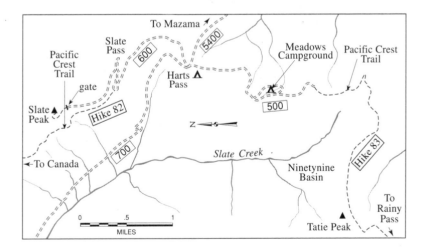

The road to Slate Peak

The path drops gently downhill below Slate Peak and in less than 2 miles brings views of the old mining complex in Barron. All the buildings you see in the basin below the trail are on private mining claims, many of which have not been worked for decades. Note how slowly the mining wounds on the meadows have healed.

It's the steep meadows along the trail, however, with their flowers, flowers, and flowers, that truly make any walk here for any distance worth the effort and the time.

To reach the top of Slate Peak, the highest point (7,440 feet) in the state reached by a road, drive beyond the switchback on Road 600 (see above) to a gate below a formal viewpoint at the top. The mountain was flattened by the Army for a radar station after World War II.

Vistas here of the Cascade Crest both north and south. Displays identify surrounding peaks.

83 Tatie Peak Ridge

Features: high vistas and meadows
One way: 2 miles or more
Elevation gain: 600 feet
Difficulty: easy to steep
Open: midsummer
Maps: Green Trails 50; Okanogan National Forest map

Follow the Pacific Crest Trail for a spectacular mile or two to sweeping vistas over open alpine meadows.

From the west, drive east on North Cascades Highway 20 over Rainy and Washington passes into the Methow Valley and turn north (left) off the highway to Mazama, less than 2 miles east of the Early Winters Information Center.

Turn left in Mazama and follow the narrow and steep Harts Pass Road 5400 for 18.5 miles to Harts Pass. At the pass turn south on Spur Road 500 and follow it to the end beyond Meadows Campground. (See map on page 178.)

At the trailhead take the Pacific Crest Trail to the left as it climbs around the edge of a ridge above a once-upon-a-time private mining site and then turns north (still climbing) to a narrow ridge extending to Tatie Peak.

Truly breathtaking views from the ridge at 7,000 feet over Ninetynine Basin to the north and over the south fork of Trout Creek to the south. And in both directions: far, far beyond. Use an Okanogan National Forest map to identify the surrounding peaks.

Pause here, certainly, and if you have the time, walk toward Tatie Peak. Just for the pleasure of it.

Pacific Crest Trail on Tatie Peak Ridge

84 Sullivan's Pond

Features: pond and birds
One way: ½ mile at most
Elevation gain: none
Difficulty: no formal trails
Open: spring to fall
Maps: Green Trails 52, 84

A wander here around a small but busy bird-filled marshy pond. Best in the spring.

On I-5 north of Mount Vernon, turn east at Exit 230 onto North Cascades Highway 20 and continue to Winthrop, following signs from there north to Pearrygin Lake State Park at the eastern end of Pearrygin Lake. From the park entrance road, drive north about 0.2 mile. Turn left at a Y and find the unsigned pond on the left in less than 2 miles as the road suddenly climbs out of the dry, open slopes and enters forest.

(On the way up enjoy the sweeping views back over Pearrygin Lake and out over Chewuch Valley ranches to the west from the road. Watch, too, for northern harriers, red-tailed hawks, and, with luck, a golden eagle.)

At the pond find an unmarked parking area on the left as

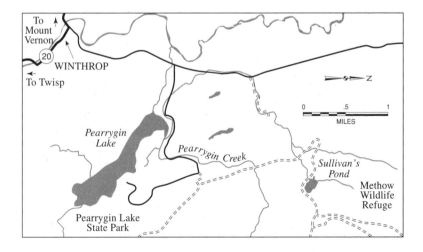

Sullivan's Pond

you reach it, another one below the road midpond, and a third at the far end of the pond in a camplike parking spot below the road as it leaves the pond. All in the Methow Wildlife Refuge.

The best walking area is on the far side of the pond off the camplike parking area along an old road through open forest near the pond. Three-strand fences mark cattle grazing allotment boundaries here. Otherwise, pick a waiting spot—and wait.

But no matter where you stop, be patient. This small pond is a world of birds and animals that will show themselves only when they are ready. In the spring, red-wing and yellow-headed blackbirds, ducks of several sorts, coots, warblers, and, in the open forest around the pond, woodpeckers, ruffed grouse, nighthawks, and swallows, to begin. And with the best of luck, deer grazing in the trees and muskrats and beavers in the pond.

85 Falls Creek Falls

Features: waterfalls
One way: less than ½ mile
Elevation gain: 75 feet
Difficulty: moderate to steep
Open: spring to fall
Map: Green Trails 52

A short walk leads to a couple of frothy, talkative, and pretty waterfalls with rock ledges for viewing.

On I-5 north of Mount Vernon, turn east at Exit 230 onto North Cascades Highway 20 and continue to Winthrop, 89 miles past Marblemount.

From Winthrop drive north on East Chewuch River Road (follow Pearrygin Lake signs out of town) along the east side of the Chewuch River. In about 6 miles turn left and cross the river to paved Road 51. Falls Creek and Falls Creek Campground are to the right in about 5.5 miles.

Find the waterfalls off a path that starts across the road from the campground, north of Falls Creek. The path continues uphill, to the right, beyond the first torrent to the second falls and then uphill on a steep scrabble trail to a viewpoint over the valley from a rock ledge.

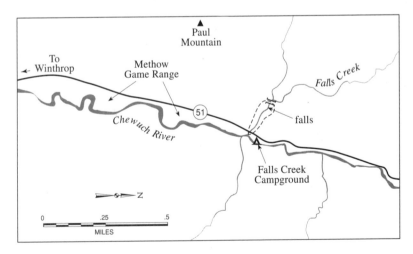

Cross a bridge when you return to walk the path on the south side of the creek.

Pretty, even in the fall. Violent in the spring.

Falls Creek Falls

Freezeout Ridge

86 Freezeout Ridge

Features: high meadow and vistas
One way: 2 miles or more
Elevation gain: 800 feet or more
Difficulty: steep to very steep
Open: summer
Map: Green Trails 53

Hike about a mile (the elevation here at near 7,000 feet will make it seem much longer) to open meadows below Tiffany Mountain, once a lookout site at 8,242 feet.

On I-5 north of Mount Vernon, turn east at Exit 230 onto North Cascades Highway 20 and continue to Winthrop, 89 miles past Marblemount.

From Winthrop drive north on East Chewuch River Road (follow Pearrygin Lake signs out of town) along the east side of the Chewuch River. In about 8 miles bear right (before reaching the Chewuch River bridge) onto Road 5010. Turn right in another mile onto Road 37.

In another 13 miles bear left onto Road 39 (Road 37 continues east to Conconully), reaching Freezeout Pass and the trailhead at 6,500 feet in about 4 more miles.

(If you can spare a moment, stop en route at the primitive campground on Roger Lake, less than a mile from the pass, to observe the work of beavers. Note the trees standing in water now. Observe fresh repairs on small dams on creeks near the campground. And notice the overgrown ridges of dams built long ago. Beaver are credited with expanding the lake to the present size you'll observe from Freezeout Trail.)

At Freezeout Pass find the ridge trail uphill to the right as it climbs steeply through toppled snags up what was once a road of some sort. Vistas down on Roger Lake from a spur path leading right in a saddle in about ¾ mile.

The path reaches the low end of the meadow system dotted with clusters of alpine fir in about a mile. The flowers here at 7,000 feet barely peek above the grass.

Cairns mark unrutted sections of the path as it makes its way toward Tiffany Mountain. If you want, continue from here on a trail up to Whistler Pass around the right side of the mountain, or pick your way slowly up the open slopes to the summit. Or—the best idea yet—find a slab of rock and enjoy the meadow with its flowers, hawks, golden eagles (if you're lucky), deer, and vistas toward the Cascade peaks—from more than 7,000 feet.

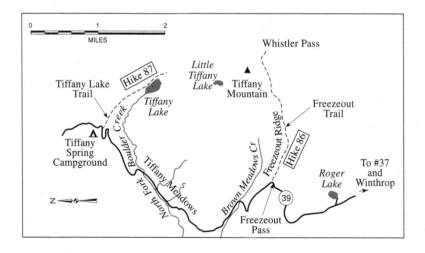

87   Tiffany Lake

Features: lake and meadows
One way: less than 2 miles
Elevation gain: 100 feet
Difficulty: easy
Open: summer
Map: Green Trails 53

An easy downhill walk on a sometimes soggy trail leads to a pretty lake with views of Tiffany Mountain.

On I-5 north of Mount Vernon, turn east at Exit 230 onto North Cascades Highway 20 and continue to Winthrop, 89 miles past Marblemount.

From Winthrop drive north on East Chewuch River Road (follow Pearrygin Lake signs out of town) along the east side of the Chewuch River. In about 8 miles bear right (before reaching the Chewuch River bridge) onto Road 5010 and turn right in another mile onto Road 37.

In another 13 miles bear left onto Road 39 (Road 37 continues east to Conconully), crossing Freezeout Pass in 4 miles and reaching Tiffany Spring Campground in another 4. (See map on page 187.)

Find the trailhead across the road from the campground. The path leads gradually downhill to the lake in about a mile and then along the lake and through a soggy marsh.

Fishing here, for sure. Marsh flowers when in season, too. And views up at Tiffany Mountain.

At the end of the marshy area, the trail climbs steeply around the backside of the mountain to Tiffany Pass and then drops back to Freezeout Pass. A stiff and sometimes precarious 6½-mile trip.

Tiffany Lake

88 Lookout Mountain

Features: grand vistas from 5,518 feet
One way: 1½ miles
Elevation gain: 1,200 feet
Difficulty: steep
Open: summer
Map: Green Trails 54

A lookout, naturally, on a mountain of the same name. With sweeping vistas over Twisp, the Methow Valley, the Columbia Basin, and all the surrounding ridges and peaks.

On I-5 north of Mount Vernon, turn east at Exit 230 onto North Cascades Highway 20 and continue to Marblemount and then 105 miles more over Washington Pass to Twisp.

In Twisp drive west on the Black Pine–Twisp River Road, turning uphill to the left in about 0.2 mile onto paved Road 200, signed "Lookout Mountain Trail." Limited views of the valley on the way to the trailhead at the end of the road in about 8 miles.

The trail makes its way uphill for less than 1½ miles, ultimately topping out on a ridge and climbing sharply to the left another ¼ mile to the lookout, staffed sometimes in the summer. And don't ask for a drink of water. Those in the tower have to carry theirs, too.

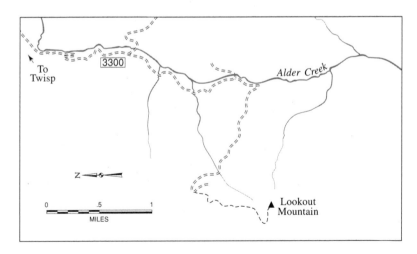

Lookout on Lookout Mountain

89 Skyline Divide

Features: meadows and vistas
One way: 2 miles
Elevation gain: 1,400 feet
Difficulty: steep
Open: summer
Map: Green Trails 13

A 2-mile hike up a forested trail brings its final reward: a tremendous view of Mount Baker, Mount Shuksan, and Excelsior Ridge from a flower-in-season alpine ridge at about 5,900 feet.

Turn east off I-5 at Exit 255 in Bellingham onto Mount Baker Highway 542 and drive about 0.5 mile east of the Glacier Public Service Center, turning south on Glacier Creek Forest Road 39. Then, in about 300 feet, turn east on Deadhorse Forest Road 37, driving about 12 miles to the trailhead parking area. Views here over the Nooksack Valley toward Excelsior Ridge and Church and Bearpaw Peaks.

The trail climbs sharply through the forest with the first views out in about a mile and the first meadows in 2 miles at about 5,800 feet. You'll be tempted to continue toward the mountain and the end of the trail in another 1½ miles. But the flower

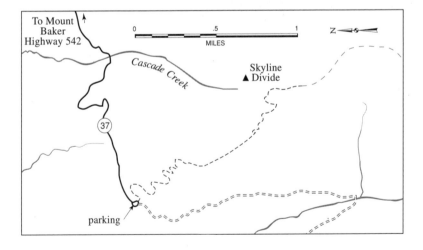

Mount Baker from Skyline Ridge

meadows (in early summer) or huckleberry meadows (in the fall) and all of their accompanying vistas remain pretty much the same now no matter how far you go—with Mount Baker all the time. Grand. Grander. Grandest.

So take time for lunch, to read, to nap. To enjoy the pleasures of a flower, observe the marmot's den, watch fairy figures in the clouds. Or just wander, aimlessly.

And there's space for everyone. You can't get lost—except in your deepest private thoughts.

Mount Baker from Excelsior Pass

 90 **Excelsior Ridge**

Features: small lakes and big vistas
One way: 3 miles
Elevation gain: 1,100 feet
Difficulty: moderate
Open: late spring to early fall
Map: Green Trails 13
Note: Check to see whether or not road is open before leaving

Hike past two pretty tarnlike lakes, through forest, and across lush meadows to a high ridge that overlooks the best of everything.

From I-5 at Bellingham turn east at Exit 255 to Mount Baker Highway 542 and north about 2 miles east of the Glacier Public Service Center, just beyond the Douglas Fir Campground, onto Canyon Creek Forest Road 31. Drive to the marked and developed trailhead near the end of the road in about 15 miles.

(On Road 31, search for leaf-imprinted rocks alongside the road just short of the 4-mile marker. Black crumbly rocks contain matted fossils of ancient stems and stalks.)

The trail to the ridge starts out in a clearcut, quickly enters forest, and soon skirts the two small Damfino Lakes. Trail bikes are supposed to turn left here for other trails to the north. You turn right and follow a hiker trail uphill through more forest, crossing several meadows and dropping slightly before climbing to Excelsior Pass at 5,300 feet.

Explosive vistas here of Baker, Church, and Bearpaw peaks and the endless clearcut blotches in the forests of Canyon Creek basin.

Hike up the knoll to the east to a former lookout site at 5,700 feet, follow the ridge trail east, or simply wander the open meadows as you wish to find your own personal observation, rest, or luncheon spot.

From the pass, trails drop down the mountain to the highway (4½ miles) or wander eastward along the ridge to Welcome Pass (4½ miles) and, again, down to the highway.

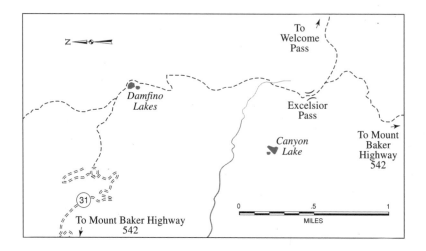

91 Twin Lakes

Features: lakes, meadows, vistas
One way: about 2½ miles
Elevation gain: 1,600 feet
Difficulty: moderate
Open: midsummer
Map: Green Trails 14

For many this hike is only a beginning, but as a short hike it's a worthy end itself.

A sometimes gated county road provides the trail. But the ugliness of the road disappears once you start toward the plateau that cradles two crystal lakes.

From I-5 at Bellingham turn east at Exit 255 to Mount Baker Highway 542. Turn north 13 miles east of the Glacier Public Service Center onto Forest Road 3065, just uphill beyond the highway maintenance barns at Shuksan. The forest road ends in about 4.5 miles near the Tomyhoi Lake trail. Best to park here and walk. The now-county road is deeply rutted and not maintained. Unworthy even to be called a trail.

But you'll soon forget it, for the vistas get better with every step. Once the "road" reaches the lakes at 5,200 feet: Heaven.

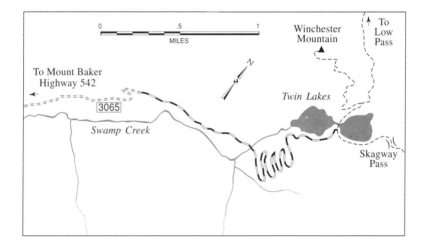

Mount Baker from Twin Lakes

Pure heaven. Crystal lakes amid heather meadows surrounded by mountain peaks.

All sorts of places for pleasant wandering and resting here. Paths this way and that. There's even a picnic table or two.

One trail, to High/Low Pass, climbs north between the lakes, ending in 4 miles at an abandoned mine. Within ¼ mile, another trail climbs west another 1½ miles to Winchester Mountain Lookout, where vistas end just short of heaven.

But it's not necessary to go the entire way on any trail here. A short walk beyond Low Pass leads across flower meadows to views of peaks beyond the Canadian border to the north. And although the lookout on Winchester Mountain is a worthy goal, a walk even partway offers views back down on Twin Lakes and more flower meadows, too.

Other paths lead east to Skagway Pass and the mining sites for which the now-closed road was built.

Warning: On all these trails steep patches of summer snow can be dangerous. *Unless you are properly equipped, turn back.*

92 Ptarmigan Ridge

Features: high meadows and wide vistas
One way: 2 miles
Elevation gain: 400 feet going in, 150 feet returning
Difficulty: moderate
Open: midsummer
Map: Green Trails 14

You can't avoid the sense of mountains here. Steep flower meadows, rock-strewn slopes, huckleberries, marmots whistling everywhere. And snow-capped mountains no matter where you turn. Nature commands these slopes and meadows. Humans have a right to visit only as guests.

From I-5 in Bellingham turn east at Exit 255 to Mount Baker Highway 542. Drive 67 miles to the end of the paved highway in a huge parking lot at Artist Point, on Kulshan Ridge at 5,100 feet, 2 miles beyond and above the Mount Baker ski complex.

The broad trail drops down from the parking lot and proceeds the first easy mile into the Mount Baker Wilderness across a sloping meadow stuffed with flowers (find the shy magenta paintbrush here). Allow time to whistle at the marmots, tempt the chipmunks, and chatter with the pikas that scamper through the rocks.

At the trail junction (Chain Lakes to the right), continue straight ahead to crest the saddle and follow the trail downhill

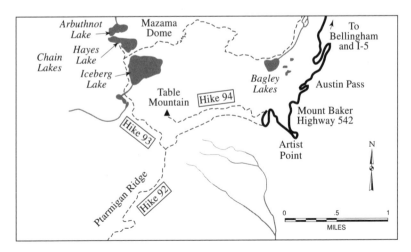

Mount Shuksan from Ptarmigan Ridge

across scree and rocks toward Ptarmigan Ridge, noting as you go
that even in these tumbled broken stones small flowers grow.

In another mile the trail climbs the ridge to camping and picnic spots on huckleberry and heather meadows. Plus vistas, yes,
that never seem to end.

The way continues another 3½ miles to an unmarked climbers' camp. (Snow sometimes covers this ridge trail all summer
long, so judge your skills and equipment before you proceed.)

If you can, walk at least another mile. The changing spectacle will take your breath away. Mount Baker, Coleman Pinnacle, Mount Shuksan, with other distant mountains everywhere.

And all through dwarf huckleberry meadows in the fall,
flowers in late spring and summer, snow patches year-round,
and heather everywhere.

93 Chain Lakes

Features: lakes, meadows, mountains
One way: 1¾ miles
Elevation change: drop 500 feet and climb 100 feet going in, the
  opposite coming out
Difficulty: steep in places
Open: midsummer
Map: Green Trails 14

A cluster of mountain lakes set in subalpine forests amid heather and huckleberry meadows—all part of, but away from, the dominating mountains in the Mount Baker Wilderness and nearby North Cascades National Park.

From I-5 in Bellingham turn east at Exit 255 to Mount Baker Highway 542. Drive some 67 miles to the end of the paved highway in a huge parking lot at Artist Point, on Kulshan Ridge at 5,100 feet, 2 miles beyond and above the Mount Baker ski complex. (See map on page 198.)

The broad trail drops from the parking lot and proceeds the first easy mile toward the mountain across steep flower meadows filled with marmots, chipmunks, and pikas scampering in the rocks, with views of Mounts Baker and Shuksan from every point along the way.

At the trail junction at the end of the steeply sloping meadow, take the trail to the right over a 5,200-foot ridge to Chain Lakes. (The trail straight ahead goes to Ptarmigan Ridge.)

The trail drops a mile through several small meadows filled with tiny private streams before climbing slightly to Iceberg Lake at 4,500 feet. Some years you will find ice floating on Iceberg Lake all summer long.

Stop here or press on to Hayes and Arbothnot lakes, only a short way farther on. To see Hayes Lake either turn right on the trail that loops back to the ski area in 4 ¾ miles or walk straight ahead on a path that proceeds on to Arbothnot Lake.

Prowl all the lakes and then return the way you came—unless you want to struggle steeply up and down to the highway at the ski area.

Mount Baker from Iceberg Lake

94   Table Mountain

Features: alpine vistas, vistas, vistas
One way: 1 mile
Elevation gain: 600 feet
Difficulty: steep all the way
Open: mid- to late summer
Map: Green Trails 14

You'll need persistence here for sure. There are few flat sections on this trail. And as you go up, no going down at all.

But every effort, every promise to yourself to never come this way again, will be forgotten in the end. For what you see and remember here will overwhelm every moment's pain.

From I-5 in Bellingham turn east at Exit 255 to Mount Baker Highway 542 and drive some 67 miles to the end of the paved highway in a huge parking lot at Artist Point, on Kulshan Ridge at 5,100 feet, 2 miles beyond and above the Mount Baker ski complex. (See map on page 198.)

The trail starts behind a sign on the uphill side of the parking area and then switchbacks steadily and steeply to the top of the mountain.

Let all speedy hikers pass, remembering: The fabled turtle beat the rushing hare.

But even if the grade presents no pain, this is not a trail to hurry up but to stop on often to view the enormous scenes that spread out before you in ever-changing modes.

And take time, too, to explore short spur trails to other vistas and sometime-tarns and to enjoy the flowers in the summer and huckleberries in the fall (if you manage to get there before others have picked them all) before settling down to the switchbacks that climb up and across the rocky slope. You'll need to use your compound lower gear on stretches here for sure.

And take no shortcuts either going up or coming down. A loose rock can pose a danger not only to you but to those on the trail below you if it should fall.

At the top veer to the left to wend your way less strenuously now across the Table's top.

For most hikers the top of the plateau at 5,700 feet will be the final goal. So once there, relax, wander, look around. Rest

Mount Shuksan from Table Mountain

atop a boulder here, run your fingers through the mountain heather there. Find a huckleberry (if it's fall) in the little bushes at your feet. And wonder how a flower could possibly grow on that rock over there.

The trail continues across and down the backside of the mountain. But unless your mountain judgment is good, return the way you came. The trail down the mountain there is steep all the time, can be risky in spring, and unsafe always when snow is on the path.

And never forget your binoculars and camera here, whether you plan to hike to the first ledge or the last. In addition to vistas: Scurrying pikas, whistling marmots, and wild flowers at every turn.

Mount Baker from Artist Ridge

95 Fire and Ice and Artist Ridge

Features: alpine environmental displays
One way: Fire and Ice, ½ mile; Artist Ridge, 1 mile
Elevation gain: modest
Difficulty: easy (wheelchair access)
Open: midsummer
Maps: Green Trails 14; Forest Service Heather Meadows map

Defined samples here of the best in alpine vistas, plants, animals, and geology. All from two easy loop trails near the end of Mount Baker Highway 542, but with enormous weekend crowds since the old rough gravel road was paved beyond the ski complex.

From I-5 in Bellingham turn east at Exit 255 to Mount Baker Highway 542 and drive some 67 miles to the Mount Baker ski complex.

Fire and Ice Trail. Find the trail off a parking lot to the right (west) of the highway near Austin Pass (4,700 feet) beyond the visitor center and ski complex where the road starts its sharp uphill climb to Artist Point on Kulshan Ridge.

You'll find no views here of Mount Baker or Mount Shuksan to divert you. Here, tucked in a valley below Table Mountain and Mount Herman, you'll have time to study the flowers along the trails, to identify the pikas, ravens, hawks, and chipmunks living here, and to consider the geology that shaped the basin.

The path starts out across slopes of up-ended columnar basalt, ground by glaciers into a classic honeycomb floor, and then wanders beside other bent and twisted columns stacked vertically like a fence.

Weathered and stunted mountain hemlock stand like strangers in the meadows here. Many of these stunted trees—thick at the bottom, small at the top, and not very tall because they've had so little time in the short alpine summers to add growth anywhere except near their roots—are more than 700 years old.

Follow the paved trail, designed for wheelchairs, downhill off the parking lot to displays overlooking Bagley Lakes. (A shorter paved loop at the beginning of the trail provides a less arduous wheelchair loop.)

From the lake overlook, a gravel trail leads to the left and

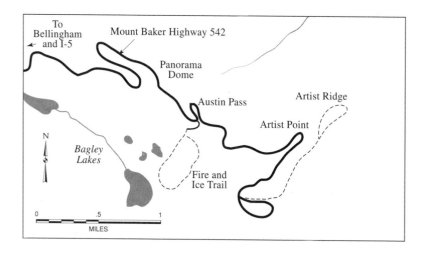

circles gradually back up to the parking area along a little stream through heather and huckleberry meadows filled with avalanche lilies in the early summer and yellow alpine monkey flowers near small streams in the fall.

Unmarked trails lead down from the overlooks to the lake and other trails that cross the basin to Chain Lakes and the Austin Pass picnic area.

Formal displays explain most of the features along the way. And early in the summer, watch for skiers on the steep slopes to the west and south.

Artist Ridge Trail. Find the trail off the huge parking lot (5,100 feet) at the end of the highway. This hike offers a prime sample of a barren alpine terrain touched here and there with flowered and heathered patches of earth all guarded by alpine trees.

The trail starts to the right of the restroom at the entrance to the parking area. A paved path for wheelchairs leads to the first display. Gravel paths and rock steps lead around the rest of this truly alpine loop. Mount Shuksan and Mount Baker are constant companions here with mountains in Canada looking over ridges to the north.

Here, too, printed displays explain the geologic forces that shaped this rocky point and identify the plants, birds, and animals to be seen along the trail.

Near the end, the trail winds past little tarns and a point overlooking Swift Creek valley to a pond and a quotation from Aldo Leopold: "... sit quietly and listen, think hard of everything you've seen, and try to understand...."

Austin Pass visitor center and ski complex

96
Esmeralda Basin

Features: high meadows and wildflowers
One way: 2-plus miles
Elevation gain: 1,200 feet
Difficulty: easy to steep
Open: midsummer
Map: Green Trails 209

Start with a rock-shredded waterfall and then hike into flower meadows that offer fresh bouquets for each new week in summer. And one weekly bouquet—truly—is no better than another.

Drive east on I-90 to Cle Elum and turn off at Exit 85 to Blewett Pass Highway 970/97. In about 6 miles turn left onto Teanaway Road (later Road 9737). Follow it to the end, about 22 miles from Highway 970. Find parking spots and picnic tables below the falls at the road-end.

The path starts to the right of the series of waterfalls (each short sidetrip to the river's edge brings a different view). Above the falls the path makes its way sharply upstream in a long ½ mile to a junction. Turn left at a fork with Lake Ingalls Trail.

Bear ahead now on an old mining road to an unmarked point in about ¼ mile where the main trail turns to the right and climbs to a higher level on the slope and an older path proceeds

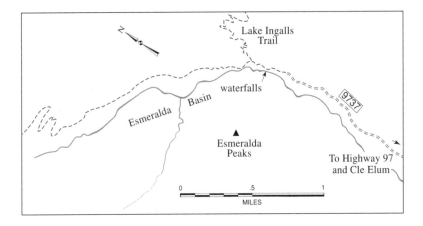

ahead. Take either one. Or go up one and back the other, for both end at the head of the valley at about 5,200 feet.

Flowers here grow in all sorts of environments. Some bloom wildly on bone-dry slopes. Others literally explode in marshy spots. Sometimes you'll find both of them, side by side.

The lower path makes its way on a soggy, unkept, and unmarked trail along the old road through a series of meadow pockets crowded with wet-rooted flowers.

The upper, more developed path, just as interesting, climbs uphill through drier slopes and different flowers but with occasional soggy patches, too.

The trails join at the head of the valley in less than 2 miles in an open area where miners—and sometimes hikers—camp. Look up at diggings on the slopes. The path continues up the ridge to the right, leaving all the flowers behind.

Don't forget your flower book and camera, and as you hike look up at the ridges for goats and, in the spring, for more waterfalls.

Scarlet gilia

Mount Rainier from Lion Rock

97 Lion Rock

Features: high vistas
One way: as far as you like
Elevation gain: slight
Difficulty: unmarked but easy
Open: summer
Map: Green Trails 210

Stand on the rim of a massive ridge of basalt and look from 6,200 feet down into the Swauk Valley and out at Enchantment Peaks, Mount Stuart, and Mount Rainier—to the sound of coyotes in the gulches far below.

Drive east on I-90 to Cle Elum and turn off at Exit 85 onto Highway 970/97 leading to Wenatchee. At Blewett (formerly

Swauk) Pass, turn right onto Road 9716, and in about 3 miles turn left onto Road 9712 to a junction with Road 35. Turn right (south) on Road 35, driving another 4 miles to turn right again onto an unmarked spur road that leads past the small, primitive Lion Rock Spring Campground and spring and on to a viewpoint and the old Lion Rock lookout site in another 0.75 mile.

As you travel Road 35, much of it above 6,000 feet, stop at unmarked but obvious vista points on the west (right) side of the road. Wander here, too, if you wish. And be sure to note the stunted flowers that struggle on all of the ridges here.

(For a more scenic but more complex route to Lion Rock with views over the Ellensburg countryside from every hairpin turn, take I-90 Exit 85 and follow Highway 970 to its junction with Highway 97. Turn a hard right onto Highway 97 and in 8 miles left onto Smithson Road. Drive east another 3.75 miles and turn left onto Road 35, following it from about 2,000 feet to its paved and gravel end at more than 6,000 feet. Turn left to Lion Rock in another 0.25 mile. Open meadows and grander vistas the higher you drive.)

At Lion Rock wander where you wish along the edge of the cliff. Jeep paths to the south. Pick your own way to the north through more flowers struggling to make it with little water in a so-short growing season.

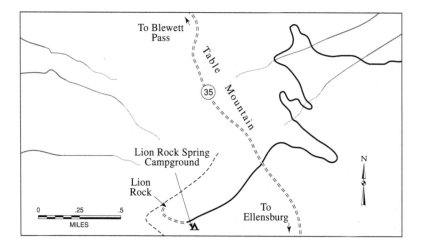

98 Naneum Meadows

Features: high meadows, springs, basalt cliffs
One way: 1½ miles
Elevation loss: 500 feet
Difficulty: moderate to easy
Open: summer
Map: Green Trails 210

Only a small sample here of the high plateaus in the Wenatchee Mountains southwest of Wenatchee: meadows, flowers, bursts of basalt, springs, spurts of forest, and ancient ponderosa pines.

Drive east on I-90 to Cle Elum and turn off at Exit 85 onto Highway 970/97 leading to Wenatchee. At Blewett (formerly Swauk) Pass, turn right onto Road 9716, and in about 3 miles turn left onto Road 9712. Pass the junction with Road 35 and find the trailhead to the right downhill in little more than a mile.

(To be picked up at the lower end of the trail, have your driver return on Road 9712, turning left on Road 35 and left again in a half mile onto Road 3530. Find the exit of the trailhead in about 2 miles, downhill on the left.)

The trail starts at the top at 5,600 feet through sage and lupine meadows and drops shortly into forest and around a spring

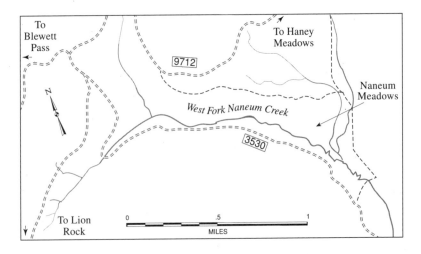

fenced for cattle. Keep right here but generally straight ahead as the trail grows faint, picking up blazes on trees beyond the clearing.

Note the snags of great old ponderosa pines and Douglas fir as the path joins a wider trail from the left before dropping to Naneum Creek and Trail 1381.

As you drop downhill note the dusting places for cows and elk beneath the trees and wonder what a rusty old truck bumper is doing near the trail.

At the bottom take the heaviest traveled trail to the right. Places for no-fire camping here on unsigned spurs that lead into coves surrounded by mounds of basalt.

The path crosses Naneum Creek and makes its way past more ridges of basalt on one side and verdant meadows on the other.

You can see the road across the way now, so take time to wander the meadows before returning to the trail, turning right across a bridge and walking back into forest to the highway trailhead at about 5,100 feet.

The best time to walk here is early in the summer before cattle eat the flowers and muck up the paths.

Naneum Meadows

99 Red Top

Features: rock fields and vistas
One way: 1 mile or less
Elevation gain: 360 feet or less
Difficulty: moderate to very steep
Open: summer
Maps: Green Trails 209, 210

Hike to the lookout tower at 5,361 feet for vistas to be seen no place else in this area and then, on a lower trail, to an agate field that looks more like an artillery or missile target range than a meadow.

Drive east on I-90 to Cle Elum and take Exit 85 onto Highway 970/97 leading to Wenatchee. In 18 miles beyond Cle Elum, turn left off Highway 97 (about 0.1 mile beyond Mineral Springs Campground) onto Road 9738. In 2.6 miles turn left on Road 9702, driving 5 miles more to the lookout parking and picnic area.

Find the trail to both the lookout and the agate fields off a road loop above the parking area.

To reach the lookout turn uphill to the left at a trail junction in about 25 yards from the road onto a trail that climbs steeply and persistently to the lookout in, as the sign says, 1 mile, although it may be less and seem like more.

As you near the top, note the desert flowers that manage to grow in the rock scree surrounding the tower. But don't disturb

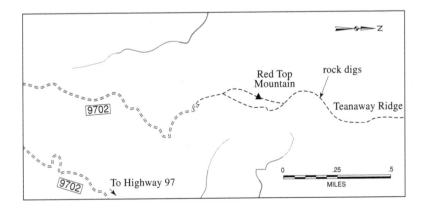

Red Top Lookout

any of the plants you see. Admire them, yes, but consider the struggle they made to gain a foothold in this barren, unstable slope and leave them for others to admire.

From the tower—on a clear day—see Rainier, Stuart, the tip of Adams, and the other peaks in the Cascades as well as the Ellensburg and Cle Elum valleys. Carry a Wenatchee National Forest map to identify most of the nearby peaks you see.

To visit the agate beds—and you really should—turn right at the junction off the parking area. The path here stays below the ridge with vistas to the east before climbing to a meadow and, immediately: The target range–looking agate bed. Spur trails to the right lead into the maze of uncovered holes dug and redug by rockhounds here for agates and thunderstones, which are, apparently, after decades of digging, still being sought and found.

A teepee-shaped outhouse erected by a rock group stands in the middle of the carnage. If you're not an expert on these stones, talk to diggers and they'll show you what they're looking for.

There's a kind of frenzy demonstrated here for sure. Yet, as you'll note, the poor trees still survive.

100 Stormy Mountain

Features: spectacular vistas from 7,200 feet
One way: 1½ miles
Elevation gain: 1,100 feet
Difficulty: steep
Open: summer
Map: Green Trails 147

Hike to a former lookout site with vistas that stretch from the wheat fields of eastern Washington, over the apple orchards of Chelan, to the Cascades as far south (on a clear day) as Mount Adams with the maw of Mount St. Helens and Glacier Peak thrown in.

Drive east on I-90 to Cle Elum and turn off at Exit 85 onto Highway 970/97 leading to Wenatchee. From Wenatchee drive north to either Entiat or Lake Chelan State Park, the simplest route being from Lake Chelan.

From Lake Chelan State Park, drive up the lake to 25 Mile Creek, turning uphill onto Road 5900 and then left in 2.5 miles onto Road 8410. Views out over Lake Chelan, Chelan, Manson, and the Columbia Basin in about 8 miles, reaching the trailhead at a saddle atop the Chelan Mountain ridge, 20 miles from the lake.

From Entiat, drive 10 miles east to Ardenvoir, turning right

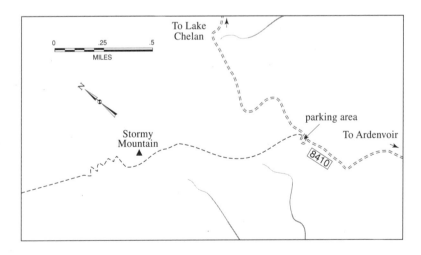

Weather-bleached trees on top of Stormy Mountain

in another 1.4 miles onto Mud Creek Road 5300 and then left in 5.9 miles more onto Road 8410, signed "Baldy Mountain." In about 4 more miles, the road climbs past a maze of unmarked, often confusing, junctions before contouring around Baldy Mountain and climbing on to the trailhead at a saddle atop the ridge, about 21 miles from Ardenvoir. (There's less confusion coming down.)

From a parking area at the saddle, the trail climbs to the west a steep ¾ mile to the junction of another steep trail from Windy Gap, leveling off after another ¾ mile just below the summit. At the highest point take a spur trail to the right through silver stumps to reach the old lookout site with a lot of places to wander and miles and miles to see.

One sad note, though: As the trailhead sign says, the trail is an example of "Your ORV dollars at work," or more truly, an example of the public's auto gas tax "hiker" money being used to reconstruct a "road" for motorcycles that are already grinding ruts in the path you paid for.

Mad River trail

101 Lower Mad River

Features: forest along a river trail
One way: 1½ miles or less
Elevation gain: slight
Difficulty: easy
Open: summer
Map: Green Trails 147

An easy and pleasant hike up a shady river canyon from Pine Flat Campground on the Mad River.

Drive east on I-90 to Cle Elum and turn off at Exit 85 onto Highway 970/97 leading to Wenatchee. From the junction of Highways 2 and 97 just west of Wenatchee, drive north on Highway 97 to Entiat in 15 miles. At Entiat turn left to Ardenvoir, another 10 miles.

In a short 0.5 mile beyond Ardenvoir, turn left onto Forest Road 5700, driving about 3 miles to a steep spur road on the left that drops down to the campground (sometimes not signed).

The trail off the uphill end of the campground follows the twisting river to Hornet Creek and beyond. Most pleasant the first mile.

Note how some of the older trees were scorched but still survived ground fires that raged through here in the past.

Watch, too, for groves of trees with which beavers once envisioned building a dam. Some trees were gnawed but never felled before the beavers abandoned whatever plans they had.

Find the junction with Hornet Ridge Trail across the river to the left in 1½ miles. And watch for rattlesnakes on the trail all along the way.

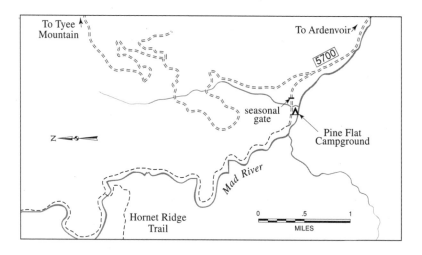

Tyee Mountain Lookout

Features: vistas and meadows from 6,600 feet
One way: as far as you wish to go
Elevation gain: slight
Difficulty: moderate, steep in spots
Open: midsummer
Map: Green Trails 147

Less than two decades ago, this lookout was best known for its view of the damage wrought by fires that swept all across the ridges seen from here.

Today, the lookout looks out on greenery again. Most of the burned snags have turned to silver or fallen, and the mountainsides and panoramas are again worthy of your time. The lookout is staffed some years.

Drive east on I-90 to Cle Elum and turn off at Exit 85 onto Highway 970/97 leading to Wenatchee. From the junction of Highways 2 and 97 just west of Wenatchee, drive north on Highway 97 to Entiat in 15 miles. Turn left to Ardenvoir in another 10 miles.

In a short 0.5 mile beyond Ardenvoir, turn left onto Forest Road 5700, driving about 15 miles before turning right uphill to Spur Road 5713. Continue another 4.2 miles over rougher road to the lookout site. (Logging some years may disrupt signing.)

From the lookout a circle of mountains here: Stuart, Rai-

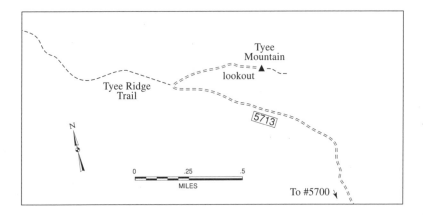

Tyee Ridge Trail

nier, Adams, Glacier Peak, and all the Cascades and the North
Cascades.

But don't stop your vista-gawking at the tower. Hike out
Tyee Ridge Trail (park at the switchback just below the tower).

First, stand there in awe of the ghost forest created by the
furnace of flame that consumed this ridge. Then note that not
every tree was destroyed in the holocaust. The few that survive
live now to reseed the slope.

And finally, note how the birds have returned. And the flowers.
The tracks of deer and the scat of smaller animals.

The trail continues more than 5 miles along the ridge. Walk
as far as the scene pleases you.

103 Big Hill

Features: vistas, old burn, forest, meadows
One way: 2 miles
Elevation gain: 400 feet
Difficulty: steep
Open: midsummer
Maps: Green Trails 114, 115, 146, 147; Wenatchee National Forest
map

Big views, as you'd expect, from a former lookout site. But special views, from a trail that crosses an old burn, climbs into old, untouched forest, and rests in high meadows.

The fire here, started by lightning in August 1970, swept the entire Silver Creek basin before being stopped by firefighters at the top of the ridge.

Drive east on I-90 to Cle Elum and turn off at Exit 85 onto Highway 970/97 leading to Wenatchee. From the junction of Highways 2 and 97 just west of Wenatchee, drive north on Highway 97 toward Entiat and turn left in 15 miles to Ardenvoir/ Entiat River Road 51. In 29 miles turn right (beyond Lake Creek Campground) to Road 5900, following it to Shady Pass (vista there) in about 8.5 miles. At the pass turn left on Road 112 and drive about 2 miles (still more vistas here) to a point where Road

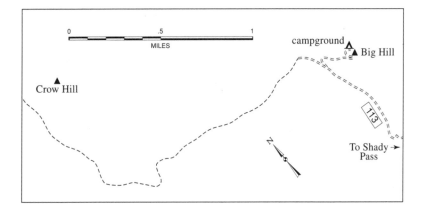

Results of 1970 fire near Chelan Mountain trailhead

112 turns sharply uphill to the right and Road 113 continues to the trailhead.

Drive or walk the steep Road 112 less than ¼ mile uphill to top of Big Hill (6,827 feet), the former lookout site, and primitive camp and cabin with mementos of the fire. The 360-degree views here include everything from Glacier Peak past Lake Chelan around to Mount Rainier and back again.

And then, once satisfied, return to Road 113 and the trail.

The path, off the left-hand side of the road-end, drops down a fireline to a saddle, becoming a trail as it climbs from the left of the saddle through a burned forest. Note as you walk here how one tree or clump of trees, all white skeletons now, was burned while another was not as the fire swept up the slope to stop at the fireline along the crest of the Chelan ridge. Note, too, how the flowers are returning and the lodgepole (always first to appear) and white pines are reestablishing themselves.

The trail soon climbs gracefully up to another saddle at nearly 7,000 feet and immediately enters a forest untouched by fire, shortly reaching patches of open meadows on the side of Crow Hill.

Take time here to walk north across a meadow to a view over Lake Chelan before continuing on the trail to still another saddle that looks toward the east.

Silver and Entiat Falls

Features: the best of waterfalls
One way: ½ mile to Silver Falls
Elevation gain: 600 feet to Silver Falls
Difficulty: easy at Entiat but steep at Silver Falls
Open: summer
Map: Green Trails 146

Two spectacular waterfalls: one you can almost stand under but have to work to get to and another you can sit beside by simply wandering to it. Both near campgrounds within about 2½ miles of each other.

Drive east on I-90 to Cle Elum and turn off at Exit 85 onto Highway 970/97 leading to Wenatchee. From the junction of Highways 2 and 97 just west of Wenatchee, drive north on Highway 97 toward Entiat and turn left in 15 miles to Ardenvoir/

Silver Falls trail

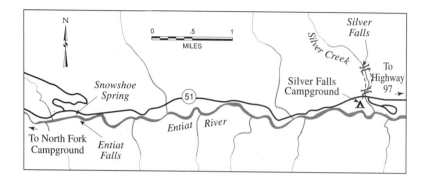

Entiat River Road 51. Reach Silver Falls in 30 miles; Entiat Falls in 32.5 miles.

Silver Falls. Find the nature trail to the series of Silver Falls on the north side of the road across from a parking area and display board at the entrance of Silver Falls Campground.

At the first fork in the trail with its formal viewing platform, turn right on a path that drops over a footbridge and then zigzags up along the tumbling creek.

Four more viewpoints offer different perspectives of the series of falls as you climb. At the first ledge go straight ahead to a cooling seat. Return to the trail and continue uphill to yet another perspective and another place to rest.

Reach the third and best viewpoint by climbing higher still below towering slabs of rock to a point almost underneath the falls. However, don't try to stand beneath the dripping cliff. The wet rocks are very slippery. Views here out over the valley, too.

The last and longest spurt of trail switchbacks up and away from the creek before returning to a bridge over a small sliding waterfall before dropping back to the first trail junction past more views over the valley and one more perspective of the falls.

Entiat Falls. Find the trail to Entiat Falls on the Entiat River to the left of the road off a parking strip. Here the path drops to a pool below the falls, which thunder over broad slabs of rock in spring and through a single cleft in the rock later in summer. In early summer watch for water ouzels (dippers) feeding chicks in niches of rock bordering the falls. Look for yellow mouths gaping from almost-hidden nest holes in dripping moss.

The falls can also be reached by trail along the river from North Fork Campground.

Appendix

Snoqualmie Pass Interstate 90

Hikes 1–5

Tinkham. 47 units in a forested campground on the south fork of the Snoqualmie River. Turn south off I-90 at Exit 42 (Tinkham Road); campground on the river side of the road. Toilets. Water. Fee.

Denny Creek. 42 units in a series of loops. Some sites near the river, others in pleasant forest. Heavily used. Turn off I-90 at Exit 45 and loop over the freeway; campground in about 2.5 miles. Group reservations. Toilets. Water. Fee.

Commonwealth. 12-unit primitive camp at Snoqualmie Pass. Turn off I-90 at Exit 52 at the pass, and loop north under the highway and then west downhill less than 0.25 mile on the old highway. Pit toilets. No water.

Hikes 6–12

Crystal Springs. 20 units between the Yakima River and I-90 off Exit 62. Sounds of the highway overpower sounds of the river. Pit toilets. Water. Fee.

Kachess. 180 units in a forested peninsula between Kachess and Little Kachess lakes. Some sites near the lake, others near Gale Creek. 5 miles north of I-90 at Exit 62. Restrooms. Water. Fee. Reservations.

Wish Poosh. 39 units on forested loops on Cle Elum Lake. 8 miles from Cle Elum on Road 903. Restrooms. Water. Swimming beach. Fee.

Cle Elum River. 35 units in pleasant, open forest near the Cle Elum River. 15 miles from Cle Elum on Road 903. Toilets. Water. Fee.

Owhi. 23 walk-in tent sites on Cooper Lake. 23 miles from Cle Elum (5 miles west of Road 903). Toilets.

Red Mountain. 12 units near the Cle Elum River. 16 miles north of Cle Elum on Road 903. Toilets.

Salmon la Sac. 127 units on forested loops, some near the river. 25 miles from Cle Elum on Road 903. Toilets. Water. Fee. Reservations.

Fish (Tucquala) Lake. 15 primitive sites in a forested area on the Cle Elum River near Tucquala Lake. 29 miles from Cle Elum on Road 903. Toilets.

Stevens Pass Highway 2

Hikes 13–15

Wallace Falls State Park. 6 walk-in, tent-only units off a parking lot. No camping facilities for trailers or campers. Always full in the summer. Restrooms. Water. Fee. Closed some days in the winter.

Troublesome Creek. 30 units on a forested loop; most sites near the river. Some equipped for wheelchair campers. Sites both east and west of the bridge. Popular on weekends. 11 miles north of Highway 2 on Forest Road 63. Pit toilets. Nature trail.

San Juan. 10 units near the north fork of the Skykomish River. About 1.25 miles beyond Troublesome Creek Campground (above). Pit toilets.

Hikes 16–20

Beckler River. 27 units on a pleasant, forested loop near, but not on, the Beckler River. 1 mile north of Skykomish. Toilets. Water. Fee.

Money Creek. 24 units, some near the river, some on forested loops. A busy camp just off Highway 2. 4 miles west of Skykomish. Toilets. Water. Fee.

Miller River. 18 units by reservation only. In old-growth timber. 3 miles south of Highway 2 on Road 6412. Toilets. Water. Designed for groups, but available to anyone for a $50 daily fee.

Hikes 21–26

For campground information, see Hikes 16–20; Hikes 27–29; and Hikes 30–34.

Hikes 27–29

Lake Wenatchee State Park. 197 units on both sides of the Wenatchee River outlet. Most sites away from the lake. An extremely heavily used area. Swimming. Boating. Restrooms. Water. Showers. Fee.

Nason Creek. 76 units on both sides of Road 6707 leading to the state park. Has been mistaken for the state park. Popular trailer area. Pit toilets. Water. Fee.

Glacier View. 20 sites in a very pleasant campground at the far end of South Shore Lake Wenatchee Road 6707. Walk-in tent sites from parking spurs on a campground loop. Some sites on the lake. Steep and narrow entrance road. No trailers. Pit toilets. Water. Fee.

Soda Springs. 5 sites in forest near the Wenatchee River. 8 miles west of Lake Wenatchee off Road 6500. Steep entrance road. No trailers. Soda spring. Pit toilets.

White River Falls. 5 units on the White River. 9 miles from Lake Wenatchee off Road 51. Waterfall attracts heavy vehicle traffic through the small camp. Steep and narrow entrance road. No trailers. Pit toilets. Water. Fee.

Note: Several other small camps can be found along Wenatchee River Road 6500 and White River Road 6400. See the Wenatchee National Forest map.

Hikes 30–34

Tumwater. 80 units in a wooded area between Chiwaukum Creek and the Wenatchee River. A popular, heavily used campground. 9 miles northwest of Leavenworth on Highway 2. Toilets. Water. Fee.

Eightmile. 45 units on loops off Icicle Creek Road 7600. About 8 miles from Leavenworth. Group reservation area. Toilets. Water. Fee.

Bridge Creek. 6 sites on Icicle Creek Road 7600. 9 miles from Leavenworth. Pit toilets. Water. Fee.

Johnny Creek. 56 units on loops north and south of Icicle Road 7600. Some near Icicle Creek. Most in pleasant forest settings. 12 miles from Leavenworth. Toilets. Water. Fee.

Chatter Creek. 12 units on forested loops above the road on two small forks of Chatter Creek off Icicle Creek Road 7600 near the Chatter Creek Ranger Station. 17 miles from Leavenworth. Pit toilets. Water. Fee.

Rock Island. 22 sites on wooded loops off Icicle Creek Road 7600. Some sites near the river. Often full. 19 miles from Leavenworth. Pit toilets. Water. Fee.

Wenatchee River County Park. 100 sites in an open, grassy area with shade trees. On the Wenatchee River. Popular. 3-plus miles east of Cashmere on the south side of Highway 2. Open all year. Restrooms. Water. Fee.

Mountain Loop Highway

Hikes 35–44

Turlow. 19 units in a wooded area across from the Verlot Information Station. Some sites near the river. Pit toilets. Water. Fee.

Verlot. 25 units in a popular campground. Generally full most weekends but pleasantly private during the week. Restrooms. Water. Fee.

Gold Basin. 80 units in another popular campground. Full most weekends. Some sites near the river but most on pleasant, forested loops. Restrooms. Water. Fee.

Red Bridge. 16 units on a forested bend in the river. Heavy trailer use. Toilets. Water. Fee.

Note: Several small camps without water and for groups by reservation can be found between Verlot and Barlow Pass.

Hikes 45–48

Squire Creek. 34 well-developed units in old forest. Some sites near Squire Creek. A Snohomish County park. 4 miles west of Darrington on Highway 530. Restroom. Water. Fee.

Clear Creek. 10 units between Mountain Loop Highway and the Sauk River. Tends to get heavy local use. Only 9 miles from Darrington. Pit toilets.

Whitechuck. 5 units near the confluence of the White Chuck and Sauk rivers. Just north of the White Chuck bridge. Pit toilets.

Bedal Creek. 19 units on a forested loop at the juncture of the Sauk and its north fork.

North Cascades Highway 20

Hikes 49–50

North End. 52 sites above the road on a shady slope just beyond the park entrance. Beach and recreation center on Cascade Lake just across the road. Restroom. Piped water.

Midway. 49 sites beyond the Cascade Lake Recreation Area. On wooded loops. Restrooms. Piped water.

South End. 17 sites, most near the water, at the south end of

Cascade Lake. The oldest and most popular area in the park. Generally full. Restrooms. Piped water.

Mountain Lake. 18 sites near the lake on a peninsula beyond the landing/boat launch area at the end of the road to the lake. Restrooms. Piped water.

Note: Campgrounds are often full during peak summer periods. Sites can be reserved by mail after January 1 for the period between Memorial Day and Labor Day. For current details call the state parks toll-free information line. If a "Campground Full" sign is posted at the Anacortes ferry terminal, campers are urged to turn back. There are no other public facilities on Orcas Island.

Hikes 51–54

San Juan County Park. 18 sites on an open bluff overlooking Haro Strait on the west side of San Juan Island. The only public campground on the island. From the Friday Harbor ferry terminal, drive west on Spring Street, bearing left on San Juan Valley Road, left again onto Douglas Road, and right on Bailer Hill Road. Continue generally westward on West Side Road, which overlooks the Strait, and turn inland at Limekiln Point, reaching the park above the Strait in a total of about 10 miles. Restrooms. Water. Fee.

Hikes 55–60

Bowman Bay. 24 sites on Bowman Bay north of Deception Pass. Sites on a wooded loop overlooking the bay. Often full. Summer only. Restrooms. Piped water. Fee.

Forest Camp. 230 sites on forested loops north of Cranberry Lake. Some sites open all year. South of Deception Pass. Restroom. Piped water. Fee.

Note: If you camp near Deception Pass, you may find the noise, particularly at night, unbearable. Jet fighters from the nearby naval air station sometimes sound like they may fly right through your tent.

Washington Park (Anacortes). 75 sites, many with water and electrical hookups. All in a forested area. At the end of the road west of Anacortes beyond the ferry terminal. Restrooms. Fee.

Hikes 61–66

Kulshan. 40 sites west of Upper Baker Lake Dam. A Puget Power campground. Flush toilets. Piped water. No fee.

Horseshoe Cove. 26 units in timbered area near the lake. Swimming area; no lifeguard. Piped water. Flush toilets. Concessionaire-operated. Fee.

Boulder Creek. 10 units in a wooded site along a glacial creek. Pit toilets. No fee.

Panorama Point. 13 units. Sites near water, but with little beach. Mountain views. Pit toilets. Water. Concessionaire-operated. Fee.

Park Creek. 12 units on a creek off Road 1144. Pit toilets. No fee.

Shannon Creek. 18 units in a wooded area near the lake. Most sites on wooded loops away from the lake. Pit toilets. No fee.

Hikes 67–68

Rockport State Park. 62 drive-in and walk-in tent sites on forested loops. 1 mile west of Rockport. Restrooms. Water. Nature trails. Fee.

Steelhead Park Campground. 39 sites in an open area on the Skagit River. A Skagit county park. Open all year. At Rockport. Restrooms. Water. Fee.

Hikes 69–70

Cascade Island. 15 sites along the Cascade River. A Department of Natural Resources campground on the south side of the river. Early summer to fall. About 2.5 miles from Marblemount. Pit toilets.

Marble Creek. 23 units, some along the river, others back on pleasant, forested loops. Narrow road may be difficult for trailers. 9 miles from Marblemount. Pit toilets. Fee.

Mineral Park. 4 units in a pleasant, forested grove on the east side of the north fork of the Cascade River. Loops west of the river are closed. Pit toilets.

Johannesburg Camp. Primitive hiker camp near the trailhead to Cascade Pass at the end of the road from Marblemount. Pit toilet.

Hikes 71–74

Goodell Creek. 22 units in a wooded area along the Skagit River. Open all year. Water. Toilets. Fee in summer.

Newhalem Creek. 129 units on forested loops south of the highway and across the Skagit River. Closed in winter. Nature trails. Naturalist programs. Water. Restrooms. Fee.

Colonial Creek. 164 units on wooded loops, some near the shore of Thunder Arm on Diablo Lake. Closed in winter. Nearby trails. Naturalist programs. Water. Restrooms. Fee.

Hikes 75–81

Lone Fir. 27 units on a loop near Early Winters Creek. 5 miles east of Washington Pass at 3,600 feet. Views of nearby peaks. Toilets. Water. Fee

Klipchuck. 46 units in pleasant, open pine forest. Sites above Early Winters Creek. 3 miles west of the Early Winters Information Center.

Early Winters. 13 units in dry, open forest at 2,200 feet on a flat near Early Winters Creek. 16 miles west of Winthrop near the Early Winters Information Center. Toilets. Water. Fee.

Hikes 82–83

Early Winters. 13 units in dry, open forest at 2,200 feet on a flat near Early Winters Creek. 16 miles west of Winthrop near the Early Winters Information Center. Toilets. Water. Fee.

Ballard. 7 units near the Methow River. 7 miles from Mazama. Pit toilets. Water. Fee.

River Bend. 5 units. Turn east on Road 060 about 7 miles from Mazama; campground in 1 mile. Pit toilets. Water. Fee.

Harts Pass. 3 primitive sites in the original camp. 18.5 miles from Mazama. Pit toilets. No water.

Meadows. 14 units in a pleasant loop around an open meadow at 6,300 feet. Turn south at Harts Pass 18.5 miles from Mazama onto Road 500; campground in 0.5 mile. Pit toilets. No water.

Note: Trailers are prohibited on Harts Pass Road. Trailer camping can be found at Early Winters Campground.

Hikes 84–88

Pearrygin Lake State Park. 83 units on open loops near Pearrygin Lake. 5 miles northeast of Winthrop. Restrooms. Water. Electricity. Fee.

Falls Creek. 7 units on a forested loop near the Chewuch River. On Road 51 north of Winthrop. Waterfalls nearby. Pit toilets. Water. Fee.

Flat. 9 units on Eightmile Creek. On Road 5130 off Road 51 north of Winthrop. Pit toilets. Water. Fee.

Tiffany Spring. 6 sites at the trailhead to Tiffany Lake. On Road 39 off Road 37 about 25 miles northeast of Winthrop. Pit toilets. Spring water.

Black Pine Lake. 21 units on a pretty, forested mountain lake below Buttermilk Butte. Best route is to drive 11 miles east of Twisp on Twisp River Road to Road 43, across the river to the left. Lake in nearly 8 more miles. Pit toilets. Water. Fee.

Mount Baker Highway 542

Hikes 89–96

Douglas Fir. 30 sites, some near the river in shady forest. 2 miles east of Glacier on Highway 542. May be closed during the week. Community kitchen. Restrooms. Fee.

Silver Fir. 20 sites mostly along the river. All in a forest setting. 13 miles from Glacier. Restrooms. Fee. Sandbars some years provide wading for children.

Hannegan. 6 sites in a trailhead camp for packers. 5 miles from Highway 542, at the end of Hannegan Forest Road 32.

Highway 97

Hikes 97–100

Beverly. 16 units in an open, wooded area along the north fork of the Teanaway River. Most sites oriented to the river. On Road 9737 about 17 miles from Highway 97, or 25 miles from Cle Elum. Toilets.

Mineral Springs. 12 sites at the junction of Medicine and Swauk creeks. Just off Highway 97, 3 miles north of the Liberty Guard Station, or 23 miles from Cle Elum. Toilets. Water. Fee.

Swauk. 23 sites on wooded loops below Highway 97 on Swauk Creek. Some sites near the creek, others in shady timber. Elevation 3,000 feet. Nature trail. Toilets.

Hikes 101–104

Entiat City Park. 135 units in an open area on Entiat Lake, formed behind Rocky Reach Dam on the Columbia River. Reservations. Restroom. Water. Fee.

Pine Flat. 9 units on a flat on Mad River. Off Road 5700, 5 miles northeast of Ardenvoir. Steep entrance road. Pit toilets. Water. Fee.

Fox Creek. 15 units on a tree-shaded flat on the Entiat River. All units back from the river. 27 miles east of Entiat. Pit toilets. Water. Fee.

Lake Creek. 17 units located on a bench above the river. 28 miles from Entiat. Pit toilets. Water. Fee.

Silver Falls. 31 sites on pleasant, forested loops on either side of Silver Creek. Some sites near the Entiat River. 30 miles from Entiat. Pit toilets. Water. Fee.

North Fork. 9 units at the end of the paved road just beyond Entiat Falls. About 32 miles from Entiat. Pit toilets. Water. Fee.

Cottonwood. 26 sites at the end of Road 51. 38 miles from Entiat. Pit toilets. Water. Fee.

Lake Chelan State Park. 201 sites along Lake Chelan. Popular area. 9 miles west of Chelan. Reservations. Restroom. Water. Fee.

Reading Suggestions

Wilderness Travel

Graydon, Don, ed. *Mountaineering, The Freedom of the Hills* (5th ed.). The Mountaineers Books, Seattle, WA

Manning, Harvey. *Backpacking: One Step at a Time.* Vintage Books, New York, NY

Trees and Flowers

Arno, Stephen F., and Hammerly, Ramona P. *Northwest Trees.* The Mountaineers Books, Seattle, WA

Lyons, C. P. *Trees, Shrubs and Flowers to Know in Washington.* J. M. Dent & Sons, Ltd., Vancouver, BC, Canada

Manning, Harvey. *Mountain Flowers.* The Mountaineers Books, Seattle, WA

Nature Guides

Kozloff, Eugene N. *Plants and Animals of the Pacific Northwest.* University of Washington Press, Seattle, WA

Peterson, Roger Tory. *A Field Guide to Western Birds.* Houghton Mifflin Company, Boston, MA

Whitney, Stephen R. *A Field Guide to the Cascades and Olympics.* The Mountaineers Books, Seattle, WA

Index

About the author:

E. M. Sterling has written three other books published by The Mountaineers: *The South Cascades,* a critique on the management of Northwest forests which went out of print when Mount St. Helens covered up the evidence; and two forest trail guides—*Trips and Trails 1* and *2.*

He was born and reared in the Midwest and has lived in the Pacific Northwest since the 1940s. He and his wife live in a houseboat on Seattle's Portage Bay.

About the photographer:

Photographer and writer Ira Spring's crisp, breathtaking images of the Northwest wilderness have been inspiring outdoor enthusiasts for several decades. His creative stamp can be found in more than forty books on the outdoors, including The Mountaineers' *100 Hikes in* series and the *Trips and Trails* guides. One of the Northwest's most active trail lobbyists, Spring was given the 1992 Theodore Roosevelt Conservation Award by Congressman John Miller for his volunteer efforts toward trail preservation and funding.